Good Housekeeping

soups & stews

Good Housekeeping

soups & stews

150 DELICIOUS RECIPES

HEARST BOOKS
A division of Sterling Publishing Co., Inc.

New York / London
www.sterlingpublishing.com

Good Housekeeping Credits

Rosemary Ellis **Editor in Chief**

Susan Westmoreland **Food Director**

Susan Deborah Goldsmith **Associate Food Director**

Delia Hammock **Nutrition Director**

Sharon Franke **Food Appliances Director**

Richard Eisenberg **Special Projects Director**

Marilu Lopez **Design Director**

Book Design by Renato Stanisic

**Library of Congress
Cataloging-in-Publication Data**

Good housekeeping : 150 delicious
recipes from the editors of Good
housekeeping magazine.
p. cm.
Includes bibliographical references and index.

ISBN-13: 978-1-58816-549-7 (alk. paper)
ISBN-10: 1-58816-549-3 (alk. paper)
1. Soups. 2. Stews. I. Good housekeeping (New
York, N.Y.)
TX757.G565 2007
641.8'13—dc22

10 9 8 7 6 5 4 3 2 1

Published by Hearst Books
A Division of Sterling Publishing Co., Inc.
387 Park Avenue South, New York, NY 10016

Good Housekeeping and Hearst Books are
trademarks of Hearst Communications, Inc.

www.goodhousekeeping.com

For information about custom editions, special sales,
premium and corporate purchases, please contact
Sterling Special Sales Department at 800-805-5489
or specialsales@sterlingpub.com.

Distributed in Canada by Sterling Publishing
ᶜ/ₒ Canadian Manda Group, 165 Dufferin Street
Toronto, Ontario, Canada M6K 3H6

Distributed in Australia by Capricorn Link
(Australia) Pty. Ltd.
P.O. Box 704, Windsor, NSW 2756 Australia

Manufactured in China

ISBN 10: 1-58816-549-3
ISBN 13: 978-1-58816-549-7

Cover Photos:
Front cover: Ann Stratton; Back cover, top:
Brian Hagiwara; back cover bottom, left to right:
Quentin Bacon, Alan Richardson, Brian Hagiwara
Spine: Antonis Achilleos

Interior Photos:
Alan Richardson: 39, 131, 168, 192; Ann Stratton 21,
34, 82, 85, 93, 119, 123, 150, 160, 207, 210, 227;
Antonis Achilleos: 81; Brian Hagiwara: 26, 31, 101,
132, 184, 225; Charlie Simokaitis: 44; Mark Thomas:
6, 8, 72, 105, 137, 141, 142, 144, 149, 157, 173, 180,
183, 197, 222, 229; Monica Buck: 59, 125; Quentin
Bacon: 63, 108, 158; Rita Maas: 54, 70; Sang An: 51;
Steven Mark Needham: 2, 3, 14, 67, 88, 99, 113, 114,
165, 176, 189, 200; William Steele: 47

CONTENTS

FOREWORD

Welcome to Good Housekeeping's Soups and Stews

s there anything more welcoming than the aroma of a simmering soup or stew? A staple of American kitchens since the arrival of our forebears, these heart-warming classics fit right into today's busy lifestyle, and for good reasons: They are easy to put together with whatever is on hand and in many cases require only a few ingredients; they are versatile enough to meet your family's tastes; they are usually low-fat and low-calorie; they mind themselves on the stove once assembled; they can be made ahead and taste even better when reheated; and they constitute a balanced meal that

Susan Westmoreland
Food Director,
Good Housekeeping

can be warmed and served one bowl at a time if your family doesn't all show up for dinner at the same moment. While soups and stews are a perfect choice for family fare, don't forget them when planning the menu for your next party. Invite guests to help themselves from a pot or two of simmering soup for a no-fuss get together, surround a steaming casserole of stew with bowls of easy garnishes for a stress-free buffet, or keep a pot of soup or chili simmering on the side of the grill to accompany burgers or steaks. In the *Good Housekeeping* kitchens we always say that you can tell the best recipes by the number of splashes on the page. We have selected our very favorite recipes to fill the pages of *Good Housekeeping's Soups and Stews* in the hope that you will take it into your kitchen, use it to create wonderful memories for your family and friends, and leave splashes on every page.

SIMPLY DELICIOUS
SOUPS AND STEWS

Easy to make and full of flavor, soups and stews are an American tradition that has survived through the centuries because these one-pot meals can adapt to the needs and tastes of the time, whatever they may be. In large cast-iron pots over open fires, colonists cooked whatever seafood or game they could find with any available vegetables and flavorings to provide the energy needed to survive in an unfamiliar world. A few centuries later these early combinations have become regional classics across the country. Eighteenth- and nineteenth-century immigrants brought European, Asian, and South American ingredients and recipes to our repertoire of slow-simmered sustenance. Twentieth-century conveniences such as the refrigerator, freezer, slow cooker, pressure cooker, and microwave have made a wider selection of ingredients available throughout the year and offer easier or faster methods of soup and stew preparation. Twenty-first-century innovation has led to the creation of soup and stew combinations that are in tune with the new millennium yet are as enticing and comforting as the originals that inspired them. *Good Housekeeping's Soups and Stews* brings you the best of all these possibilities: New World classics, international favorites, and the latest from today's most stylish tables. So get into the kitchen, pull out your biggest pot and a long-handled spoon, select some ingredients from your pantry and refrigerator, and start cooking.

Soup or Stew, Either One Means a Great Meal's on the Way

When you get right down to it, soups and stews have more similarities than differences. Both can be made from an infinite larder of ingredients, can provide a satisfying meal with only one pot to wash, and count on a flavorful liquid to bring out the best in each component. Making soups and stews is just about the easiest thing you can do in the kitchen. It requires very little equipment: All you'll need is a large, heavy stock pot, saucepan, or Dutch oven with a lid; a long-handled spoon; some pot holders; and a cutting board and sharp knife to prepare the ingredients. You'll probably find that everything else you need is already in your pantry or refrigerator. Preparing soups and stews doesn't require any fancy cooking techniques: Just combine the required ingredients, simmer them for the prescribed time, and don't let them burn.

Soups are loosely defined as any kind of meat, fish, or vegetables cooked and served in a generous amount of liquid. The name supposedly comes from the fact that centuries ago soups were eaten by sopping them up with bread. Soups can be abundantly filled with chunky ingredients as are chowders or gumbos; pureed to the thick, satiny smoothness of a bisque or cream soup; or completely clear like bouillon or consommé. And as for ingredients, the children's story *Stone Soup* reminds us that there is always something in the cupboard or refrigerator that can be used to make a delicious soup. Depending on their heartiness, they can be served as a first course or an entrée for lunch or dinner. While soups are usually served hot, there are some cool classics such as Vichyssoise and Gazpacho that can't be overlooked. Fruit soups are a refreshing exception to the definition. They are usually not cooked at all, provide their own flavorful liquid, and are as likely to appear on a dessert menu as on the list of starters.

Stews get their name from the cooking method that produces them—stewing. The factor that most distinguishes them from soups is the amount of liquid used. They are usually cooked in only enough liquid to cover and tenderize the ingredients. Unlike soups, stews are usually thickened and served hot with just a drizzle of sauce made from the stewing liquid. Although today stews can be made quickly with tender meats or just a variety of vegetables, they were originally made with tougher cuts of meat, poultry, or game that required a long cooking time to become tender and flavorful. Regional specialties such as the southern classic Brunswick stew or the Great Lakes region's fish boils developed from the need to feed a crowd with foods that were locally available.

Although making soups and stews is so easy it requires no prior cooking experience, as we tested these recipes in the *Good Housekeeping* kitchens we discovered some ways to make the experience faster, easier, more economical, and always satisfying. Here are our thoughts:

Plan Ahead

• While low-sodium canned broths provide an essential head start on busy evenings, a supply of homemade stock in the freezer is worth spending a few hours on a winter weekend watching it simmer.

• Keep a container in your freezer and collect small amounts of left-over vegetables, meat, poultry, broth, and vegetable cooking liquid to add to your next pot of soup. Deglaze the pan in which you cooked burgers, steaks, or chicken; cool the liquid, and add it to your frozen soup collection.

• If your garden produces a surplus of tomatoes, peppers, celery, or green onions, rinse, pat dry, chop, and freeze them in 1/2 cup amounts. Add them, still frozen, to soups and stews. Use within six months.

• For soups, sauces, and stews, puree herbs in a blender or mini food processor with a little water. Freeze them in an ice-cube tray that makes small cubes. Once frozen, store the cubes in a freezer-weight zip-tight plastic bag. (Do not use this method with rosemary; the flavor will be too concentrated.)

• When preparing soups and stews, double the recipe and freeze some for a busy evening. Cool the soup or stew in containers, uncovered, at least 30 minutes in refrigerator or until warm. Cover containers tightly; label and freeze up to three months.

Head for the Kitchen

• Read the recipe and check to make sure you have all the ingredients (or suitable substitutes) called for before you start cooking.

• The sections of beef most often used for stews and pot roasts are the round, the chuck, the foreshank, and the brisket. If your supermarket doesn't have the exact cut of beef your recipe calls for try to pick another cut from the same part of the animal. For example, if a recipe calls for a boneless round rump roast, you can use another round roast of equivalent weight, but don't substitute chuck for round because the flavor and cooking time may differ.

• Check the cooking time to make sure it fits within your schedule. You might want to prepare long-cooking soups or stews the night before, so they can be pulled from the refrigerator and warmed in a hurry the next day when you need them.

• Select a heavy cooking pot so that the soup or stew won't burn and one that will hold the volume of the soup or stew with an extra inch of bubble room at the top. A tight-fitting lid will prevent evaporation and loss of flavor.

• If you can't keep an eye on your soup or stew, plan to prepare it in a slow cooker following the manufacturer's directions or in a Dutch oven or casserole with a lid in a 325°F oven.

• To ensure the best results, always use standard measuring equipment. Don't be tempted to use tableware for measuring; use standard dry measuring cups for dry ingredients, glass measuring cups for liquids, and standard measuring spoons when measuring tablespoons and teaspoons.

• If a recipe calls for fresh herbs and you only have dried, use 1/3 of the amount listed (e.g., for 1 tablespoon of a fresh herb, substitute 1 teaspoon dried).

• When using dried herbs, be sure they are fresh. It is best to buy the smallest container of dried herbs possible, as they begin to lose flavor as soon as they are opened. Dried herbs should be used within six months of purchase.

Simmer and Serve

• Sautéing meat, vegetables, herbs, and spices gently before adding them to the cooking liquid will enhance their flavor. If they are to be added near the end of the cooking time, use a separate pan to sauté vegetables and herbs, and deglaze the pan with some of the broth so no flavor is lost.

• To brown the meat perfectly, dry the meat well with paper towels, heat a little oil until it's very hot, and add the chunks in small batches. This way, moisture can evaporate and the pieces will sear, not steam.

• Bring the liquid to a boil with the ingredients that will need the longest cooking time, then reduce the heat and cook gently until they are just tender. Then add quick-cooking vegetables and herbs, and cook just until they are tender.

• While the easiest way to remove fat from soups and stews is to chill them overnight and discard the layer of solid fat that forms on the surface, if you are in a hurry, you can remove fat from hot soup or stew by placing ice cubes or several lettuce leaves on the surface for several minutes then removing them.

• If your soup or stew is too salty, peel and quarter a potato and simmer in the soup or stew for 10 to 15 minutes; remove before serving. The potato will absorb some of the excess salt.

• Serve hot soups and stews in warmed dishes and cold soups in chilled dishes.

VEGETABLES

Miso Soup, page 17

Vegetable Broth

This broth is delicious, nutritious, and great in soups, risottos, and sauces. The optional fennel and parsnip lend a natural sweetness and an additional depth of flavor. For an Asian-flavored broth, add minced lemongrass, minced fresh ginger, or chopped fresh cilantro.

PREP: 25 MINUTES   COOK: 2 HOURS   MAKES ABOUT 6 CUPS

4 large leeks
2 to 4 garlic cloves, not peeled
13 cups water
salt
1 large all-purpose potato, peeled, cut lengthwise in half, and thinly sliced
1 small fennel bulb, trimmed and chopped (optional)
3 parsnips, peeled and thinly sliced (optional)

2 large carrots, peeled and thinly sliced
3 stalks celery with leaves, thinly sliced
4 ounces mushrooms, trimmed and thinly sliced
10 parsley sprigs
4 thyme sprigs
2 bay leaves
1 teaspoon whole black peppercorns
ground black pepper

1. Cut off roots and trim dark green tops from leeks; thinly slice leeks. Rinse leeks in large bowl of cold water, swishing to remove sand. Transfer to colander to drain, leaving sand in bottom of bowl.

2. In 6-quart saucepot, combine leeks, garlic, 1 cup water, and pinch salt; heat to boiling. Reduce heat to medium; cover and cook until leeks are tender, about 15 minutes.

3. Add potato, fennel if using, parsnips if using, carrots, celery, mushrooms, parsley and thyme sprigs, bay leaves, peppercorns, and remaining 12 cups water. Heat to boiling; reduce heat and simmer, uncovered, at least 1 hour 30 minutes.

4. Taste and continue cooking if flavor is not concentrated enough. Season with salt and pepper to taste. Strain broth through fine-mesh sieve into containers, pressing on solids with back of wooden spoon to extract liquid; cool. Cover and refrigerate to use within 3 days, or freeze up to 4 months.

Each cup: About 19 calories, 1g protein, 4g carbohydrate, 0g total fat (0g saturated), 0mg cholesterol, 9mg sodium.

Miso Soup

A light, spicy broth brimming with fresh vegetables and chunks of nutritious tofu.

PREP: 25 MINUTES   COOK: 35 MINUTES

MAKES ABOUT 9 1/2 CUPS OR 6 MAIN-DISH SERVINGS

1 tablespoon vegetable oil
2 large carrots, peeled and thinly sliced
2 garlic cloves, minced
1 small onion, cut into 1/4-inch pieces
1 tablespoon grated, peeled fresh ginger
1/2 small head napa cabbage (Chinese cabbage), about 1/2 pound, cut crosswise into 1/2-inch-thick slices (about 4 cups)

1/4 teaspoon coarsely ground black pepper
1 tablespoon seasoned rice vinegar
6 cups water
1 package (16 ounces) firm tofu, drained and cut into 1/2-inch cubes
1/4 cup red miso (see note), diluted with 1/4 cup hot tap water
2 green onions, trimmed and sliced

1. In 5-quart Dutch oven, heat oil over medium heat. Add carrots, garlic, onion, and ginger and cook, stirring occasionally, until onions are lightly browned, about 10 minutes.

2. Add cabbage, vinegar, pepper, and water; heat to boiling over high heat. Reduce heat to low; cover and simmer until vegetables are tender, about 20 minutes.

3. Stir in tofu and miso; heat through, about 2 minutes. To serve, sprinkle with green onions.

Each serving: About 185 calories, 14g protein, 13g carbohydrate, 10g total fat (1g saturated), 0mg cholesterol, 510mg sodium.

Note: Miso comes in a variety of flavors, colors, and textures that fall into three basic categories: red, which has a strong flavor; golden, which is mild; and white, which is mellow and slightly sweet. Miso can be purchased in health-food stores and Asian markets.

Mushroom-Barley Miso Soup

Simmer meaty shiitake mushrooms, creamy barley, and vegetables in a broth made with miso.

PREP: 20 MINUTES   COOK: ABOUT 1 HOUR

MAKES ABOUT 10 CUPS OR 6 MAIN-DISH SERVINGS

8 cups water, plus about 1 cup to add later
1 package (1 ounce) dried shiitake mushrooms
1 tablespoon olive oil
3 carrots peeled and cut into 1/4-inch pieces
1 medium onion, chopped
2 garlic cloves, minced
1 tablespoon grated, peeled fresh ginger

1/2 cup pearl barley
1/2 teaspoon salt
1/4 teaspoon coarsely ground black pepper
1 1/2 pounds bok choy, trimmed and chopped
6 tablespoons dark red miso
1 tablespoon brown sugar

1. In 2-quart saucepan, heat 4 cups water to boiling over high heat. In medium bowl, pour boiling water over dried shiitake mushrooms; let stand 15 minutes. With slotted spoon, remove mushrooms. Rinse to remove any grit; drain on paper towels. Cut stems from mushrooms and discard; thinly slice caps. Strain liquid through sieve lined with paper towels into 4-cup glass measuring cup. Add enough *water* to equal 4 cups; set aside.

2. In nonstick 5-quart Dutch oven, heat oil over medium heat until hot. Add carrots, onion, and mushrooms and cook until vegetables are tender, about 15 minutes. Add garlic and ginger and cook 1 minute longer.

3. Add barley, salt, pepper, reserved mushroom liquid, and additional 4 cups water; heat to boiling over high heat. Reduce heat to low; cover and simmer until barley is tender, about 40 minutes.

4. Add bok choy; heat to boiling over medium-high heat. Reduce heat to low and simmer, uncovered, until bok choy has wilted and is tender-crisp, 5 to 7 minutes, stirring occasionally.

5. With ladle, transfer ½ cup broth to small bowl. Add miso and brown sugar; stir until smooth.
6. Remove Dutch oven from heat; stir in miso mixture. (Never boil miso; its delicate flavor and nutrients will be destroyed by high heat.)

Each serving: About 170 calories, 7g protein, 29g carbohydrate, 4g total fat (0g saturated), 0mg cholesterol, 985mg sodium.

Tip: Making the Most of Miso

Miso, the intense Japanese soybean paste that punches up soups and dressings, is coming into its own in American kitchens. A little goes a long way toward adding a wonderful depth of flavor to healthy foods.

Sold in small tubs or jars at health-food stores and Asian markets, this high-protein, peanut butter–like paste is made from cooked soybeans, salt, water, and koji (a mold cultivated in a barley, rice, or soybean base) and fermented for 6 months to 3 years. The type of grain base, amount of koji, and length of fermentation affect the color (from pale golden to dark brown) and flavor—sweet, mild, salty, earthy, or meaty. Textures range from smooth to chunky.

High heat and boiling change miso's flavor, so incorporate it into a dish near the end of the cooking process. To avoid undissolved clumps, blend a few tablespoons into hot water or broth first. After stirring diluted miso into a soup or stew, heat mixture only to a simmer; serve immediately.

Store miso in the refrigerator in an airtight container for up to 1 year.

Leek Consommé with Herbs

A simple yet elegant clear soup for a light start to a big meal.

PREP: 25 MINUTES   COOK: 30 MINUTES

MAKES ABOUT 10 CUPS OR 10 FIRST-COURSE SERVINGS

6 medium leeks (about 2 pounds)
2 medium stalks celery
4 carrots, peeled
1 lemon
3 cans (14 to 14 1/2 ounces each) chicken or vegetable broth or 5 1/4 cups Chicken Broth (page 74) or Vegetable Broth (page 16)

3 cups water
1/8 teaspoon coarsely ground black pepper
1/4 cup loosely packed fresh parsley, chopped
1 tablespoon coarsely chopped fresh dill
10 lemon slices

1. Cut off roots and trim dark green tops from leeks; cut each leek lengthwise in half, then crosswise to separate green tops from white bottoms. Cut green tops crosswise into 1-inch pieces and slice bottoms crosswise into thin slices. Rinse tops in large bowl of cold water, swishing to remove sand. Transfer to colander to drain, leaving sand in bottom of bowl. Transfer tops to 4-quart saucepan. Repeat with bottoms; reserve separately.

2. Cut celery and 2 carrots crosswise into 1-inch pieces; thinly slice remaining 2 carrots crosswise on the diagonal. From lemon, with vegetable peeler, remove four strips (3" by 1") peel; squeeze 1 tablespoon juice.

3. Add celery, carrots, 2 strips lemon peel, broth, and water to saucepan with leek tops; heat to boiling over high heat. Reduce heat to low; cover and simmer 15 minutes.

4. Strain broth into large bowl, pressing down on vegetables in strainer with back of spoon to extract as much broth as possible; discard vegetables.

5. Return broth to saucepan. Add pepper, lemon juice, leek bottoms, carrot slices, and remaining lemon peel to broth; heat to boiling over high heat. Reduce heat to low; cover and simmer just until vegetables are tender, about 10 minutes.

6. Remove from heat; discard lemon peel. Stir in parsley and dill. Garnish each serving with 1 lemon slice.

Each serving: About 45 calories, 3g protein, 6g carbohydrate, 1g total fat (0g saturated), 1mg cholesterol, 405mg sodium.

Leek Consommé with Herbs

Wild Rice and Mushroom Consommé

Wild rice is really a grass, not a grain. Its deep earthy flavor is a perfect match for the woodsy taste of mushrooms.

PREP: 15 MINUTES   COOK: 50 MINUTES
MAKES ABOUT 12½ CUPS OR 12 FIRST-COURSE SERVINGS

3/4 cup wild rice
1/2 ounce dried porcini mushrooms
  (about 1/2 cup)
2 tablespoons butter or margarine
1 large shallot (2 ounces), finely
  chopped (about 1/4 cup)
6 ounces oyster mushrooms, trimmed
  and torn lengthwise into thin strips

6 ounces shiitake mushrooms, stems
  removed and caps thinly sliced
1/2 cup Madeira wine
1 carton (32 ounces) chicken broth
  or 4 cups Chicken Broth (page 74)
1/2 teaspoon salt

1. In 2-quart saucepan, heat rice and *3 cups water* to boiling over high heat. Reduce heat to low and simmer, covered, until rice is tender and most of water has been absorbed, about 45 minutes. Drain.

2. Meanwhile, in small bowl, pour *2 cups boiling water* over porcini mushrooms; let stand at least 20 minutes. With slotted spoon, remove porcini. Rinse to remove any grit, then chop. Strain mushroom liquid through sieve lined with paper towels; reserve.

3. In 6-quart saucepot, melt butter over medium heat. Add shallot and cook until soft, 3 to 4 minutes. Add oyster and shiitake mushrooms; cover and cook, stirring occasionally, until mushrooms are tender and very lightly browned, 4 to 5 minutes.

4. Add Madeira and heat to boiling over high heat; boil 1 minute. Stir in broth, salt, reserved porcini mushrooms and mushroom soaking liquid, and *3 cups water*. Reduce heat to low; cover and simmer 5 minutes. Add rice; heat through.

Each serving: About 80 calories, 3g protein, 12g carbohydrate, 3g total fat (2g saturated), 5mg cholesterol, 454mg sodium.

Hot and Sour Soup

Streamlined seasonings help get this popular Asian soup on the table in record time without sacrificing the great taste.

PREP: 15 MINUTES   COOK: ABOUT 15 MINUTES
MAKES ABOUT 8 CUPS OR 4 MAIN-DISH SERVINGS

1 tablespoon vegetable oil
4 ounces shiitake mushrooms, stems removed and caps thinly sliced
3 tablespoons reduced-sodium soy sauce
1 package (15 to 16 ounces) extrafirm tofu, drained, patted dry, and cut into 1-inch cubes
2 tablespoons cornstarch
1 carton (32 ounces) chicken broth or 4 cups Chicken Broth (page 74)

3 tablespoons seasoned rice vinegar
2 tablespoons grated, peeled fresh ginger
1 tablespoon Worcestershire sauce
1/2 teaspoon Asian sesame oil
1/4 teaspoon ground red pepper (cayenne)
2 large eggs, beaten
2 green onions, trimmed and sliced

1. In nonstick 5-quart saucepot, heat oil over medium-high heat until hot. Add mushrooms, soy sauce, and tofu and cook, gently stirring often, until liquid has evaporated, about 5 minutes.

2. In cup, with fork, blend cornstarch and *1/4 cup water* until smooth; set aside. Add broth and *3/4 cup water* to tofu mixture; heat to boiling. Stir in cornstarch mixture and boil, stirring, 30 seconds. Reduce heat to medium-low; add vinegar, ginger, Worcestershire, sesame oil, and pepper and simmer 5 minutes.

3. Remove from heat. Slowly pour beaten eggs into soup in a thin, steady stream around the edge of the saucepot. Carefully stir soup once in a circular motion so egg separates into strands. Sprinkle each serving with green onions.

Each serving: About 280 calories, 18g protein, 17g carbohydrate, 15g total fat (3g saturated), 106mg cholesterol, 1,790mg sodium.

Onion Soup with Parmesan Croutons

For the richest flavor, slow-cook leeks, shallots, and onions until tender, sweet, and golden brown.

PREP: 35 MINUTES   COOK: ABOUT 1 HOUR 15 MINUTES
MAKES 10 CUPS OR 8 FIRST-COURSE SERVINGS

1 bunch leeks (about 1 pound)
2 tablespoons butter or margarine
1 tablespoon olive oil
3 large onions (12 ounces each),
   each cut in half and thinly sliced
4 large shallots, each cut in half and
   thinly sliced
pinch dried thyme
2 tablespoons brandy
3 cans (14 to 14 1/2 ounces each)
   chicken broth or 5 1/4 cups Chicken
   Broth (page 74)

1 teaspoon salt
1/4 teaspoon coarsely ground black
   pepper
4 cups water
4 ounces French bread, cut
   diagonally into ten 3/4-inch-thick
   slices
1/4 cup coarsely grated Parmesan
   cheese

1. Cut off roots and trim dark green tops from leeks; cut each leek lengthwise in half, then crosswise into 1/4-inch pieces. Rinse leeks in large bowl of cold water, swishing to remove sand. Transfer to colander to drain, leaving sand in bottom of bowl.

2. In 8-quart saucepot, melt butter and olive oil over medium-high heat until hot. Add leeks, onions, shallots, and thyme, reduce heat to low and cook, covered, until tender and deep golden brown, 40 to 45 minutes, stirring occasionally.

3. Remove cover and increase heat to high. Add brandy and cook, stirring until browned bits are loosened from bottom of saucepot, 1 minute. Add broth, salt, pepper, and water; heat to boiling. Reduce heat to low; cover and simmer 20 minutes.

4. Meanwhile, preheat oven to 450°F. In 15 1/2" by 10 1/2" jelly-roll pan or on large cookie sheet, arrange bread slices in single layer; bake 3 minutes. Turn slices over; sprinkle tops with Parmesan cheese and bake until toasted, about 5 minutes longer. Top each serving with a Parmesan crouton.

Each serving: About 135 calories, 6g protein, 16g carbohydrate, 5g total fat (2g saturated), 10mg cholesterol, 761mg sodium.

Do-Ahead Tip: Croutons can be made up to two days ahead and stored in an airtight container. This soup reheats nicely if made the day before serving.

French Onion Soup Gratinée

French Onion Soup Gratinée

Onions, slowly cooked until deep brown and caramelized, give this welcome classic its distinctive flavor. Great for a dinner party, this recipe is easily doubled; simply cook the onions in two skillets.

PREP: 1 HOUR 10 MINUTES   COOK: ABOUT 1 HOUR 20 MINUTES

MAKES ABOUT 8 CUPS OR 6 FIRST-COURSE SERVINGS

4 tablespoons butter or margarine
2 1/2 pounds onions (about 6 medium), each cut in half and thinly sliced
1/4 teaspoon salt
1 cup dry white wine
1 can (14 to 14 1/2 ounces) chicken broth or 1 3/4 cups Chicken Broth (page 74)

1 can (14 to 14 1/2 ounces) beef broth or 1 3/4 cups Brown Beef Stock (page 116)
2 sprigs thyme
2 1/2 cups water
12 diagonal slices (1/2 inch thick) French bread
6 ounces Gruyère or Swiss cheese

1. In nonstick 12-inch skillet, melt butter over medium-high heat. Add onions and salt and cook, stirring occasionally, until onions turn golden brown, about 30 minutes. Reduce heat to medium-low and cook, stirring occasionally, until onions are very tender and deep golden brown, about 15 minutes longer.

2. Transfer onions to 4-quart saucepan. Add wine to same skillet; heat to boiling over medium-high heat. Boil until wine is reduced to 1/4 cup, 3 to 5 minutes. Add reduced wine to onions. Stir in broths, thyme, and water; cover and heat to boiling over high heat. Reduce heat to low; simmer, covered, 15 minutes.

3. Meanwhile, preheat oven to 450°F. In 15 1/2" by 10 1/2" jelly-roll pan, arrange bread in single layer; bake until golden brown and crisp, 8 to 10 minutes. Transfer bread to plate. Shred Gruyère; set aside.

4. Place six 1 1/2- to 2-cup oven-safe bowls in same jelly-roll pan. Discard thyme. Spoon soup into bowls and top each with 2 bread slices, overlapping slightly if necessary. Sprinkle Gruyère evenly over bread. Bake until cheese has melted and begins to brown, 12 to 15 minutes.

Each serving: About 415 calories, 16g protein, 43g carbohydrate, 19g total fat (11g saturated), 52mg cholesterol, 1,112mg sodium.

Broccoli and Cheddar Soup

Served with homemade multigrain bread (or a bakery loaf) and a crisp salad, this rich soup makes a satisfying meal. Use a blender, not a food processor, for an extra-smooth texture.

PREP: 35 MINUTES   COOK: 25 MINUTES

MAKES ABOUT 8 CUPS, 8 FIRST-COURSE, OR 4 MAIN-DISH SERVINGS

1 tablespoon olive oil
1 medium onion, chopped
1/4 cup all-purpose flour
1/2 teaspoon salt
1/4 teaspoon dried thyme
1/8 teaspoon ground nutmeg
coarsely ground black pepper
2 cups low-fat milk (2%)
1 can (14 to 14 1/2 ounces) chicken broth or 1 3/4 cups Chicken Broth (page 74)

1 1/2 cups water
1 large bunch broccoli (1 1/2 pounds), cut into 1-inch pieces (including stems)
1 1/2 cups shredded sharp Cheddar cheese (6 ounces)

1. In 4-quart saucepan, heat olive oil over medium heat until hot. Add onion and cook, stirring occasionally, until golden, about 10 minutes. Stir in flour, salt, thyme, nutmeg, and 1/4 teaspoon pepper; cook, stirring frequently, 2 minutes.

2. Gradually stir in milk, broth, and water. Add broccoli and heat to boiling over high heat. Reduce heat to low; cover and simmer until broccoli is tender, about 10 minutes.

3. Spoon one-third of mixture into blender; cover, with center part of lid removed to let steam escape, and puree until very smooth. Pour into large bowl. Repeat twice more with remaining mixture.

4. Return puree to same clean saucepan and heat to boiling over high heat, stirring occasionally. Remove from heat; stir in cheese until melted and smooth. To serve, sprinkle with coarsely ground black pepper.

Each first-course serving: About 185 calories, 12g protein, 12g carbohydrate, 11g total fat (6g saturated), 27mg cholesterol, 485mg sodium.

Carrot and Dill Soup

Combine sweet carrots with fresh orange, dill, and a touch of milk for a refreshing creamy soup without the cream.

PREP: 25 MINUTES   COOK: ABOUT 45 MINUTES

MAKES ABOUT 10 1/2 CUPS OR 10 FIRST-COURSE SERVINGS

1 tablespoon olive oil	1 tablespoon sugar
1 large onion (12 ounces), chopped	3/4 teaspoon salt
1 medium stalk celery, chopped	1/4 teaspoon ground black pepper
2 large oranges	4 cups water
2 bags (16 ounces each) carrots, peeled and coarsely chopped	1 cup milk
	1/4 cup chopped fresh dill
1 can (14 to 14 1/2 ounces) chicken broth or 1 3/4 cups Chicken Broth (page 74)	dill sprigs

1. In 5-quart Dutch oven, heat olive oil over medium-high heat until hot. Add onion and celery and cook, stirring occasionally, until tender and golden, about 15 minutes.

2. Meanwhile, from 1 orange, with vegetable peeler, remove 4 strips (3" by 1" each) peel and from both oranges squeeze 1 cup juice.

3. Add orange peel to Dutch oven and cook, stirring, 2 minutes longer. Add orange juice, carrots, broth, sugar, salt, pepper, and water; heat to boiling over high heat. Reduce heat to low; cover and simmer until carrots are very tender, about 25 minutes.

4. Remove orange peel. Spoon one-third of mixture into blender; cover, with center part of lid removed to let steam escape, and puree until smooth. Pour into large bowl. Repeat twice more with remaining mixture.

5. Clean Dutch oven and return puree to pan. Stir in milk and chopped dill; heat just to simmering over medium heat. Garnish each serving with a dill sprig.

Each serving: About 95 calories, 3g protein, 16g carbohydrate, 3g total fat (1g saturated), 3mg cholesterol, 335mg sodium.

Carrot and Apple Soup

Use the blender to puree this winning combination of sweet carrots and apples right in the Dutch oven. We call for Golden Delicious apples for their consistently good flavor, but feel free to substitute other varieties.

PREP: 20 MINUTES   COOK: 35 MINUTES

MAKES ABOUT 10 CUPS OR 8 FIRST-COURSE SERVINGS

2 tablespoons butter or margarine
1 large onion (12 ounces), coarsely chopped
3 medium Golden Delicious apples (1 pound)
2 pounds carrots
2 cans (14 to 14 1/2 ounces each) chicken broth or vegetable broth or 3 1/2 cups Chicken Broth (page 74) or Vegetable Broth (page 16)

1 tablespoon sugar
1 teaspoon salt
1 teaspoon grated, peeled fresh ginger
2 cups water
half-and-half or heavy cream (optional)
fresh chives for garnish (optional)

1. In 5-quart Dutch oven, melt butter over medium heat. Add onion and cook, stirring occasionally, until tender and golden, about 12 minutes.

2. Meanwhile, peel, halve, and core apples. Peel and trim carrots. Cut apples and carrots into 1 1/2-inch pieces.

3. Add apples, carrots, broth, sugar, salt, ginger, and water to onions; heat to boiling over high heat, stirring occasionally. Reduce heat to low; cover and simmer until carrots are very tender, about 20 minutes.

4. Remove from heat. Spoon one-third of mixture into blender; cover, with center part of cover removed to let steam escape, and puree until smooth. Pour into large bowl. Repeat twice more with remaining mixture.

5. Clean Dutch oven and return soup to pan. Heat through. Serve with a swirl of half-and-half and garnish with fresh chives if you like.

Each serving: About 130 calories, 2g protein, 23g carbohydrate, 4g total fat (2g saturated), 8mg cholesterol, 786mg sodium.

Carrot and Apple Soup

Harvest Mexican Soup

This soup is full of savory ingredients, including corn, avocado, and lime. The jalapeño chile adds a burst of heat.

PREP: 25 MINUTES   COOK: ABOUT 30 MINUTES

MAKES ABOUT 9 1/2 CUPS OR 6 MAIN-DISH SERVINGS

4 teaspoons olive oil

1 jumbo onion (1 pound), cut into 1/4-inch pieces

2 medium carrots, peeled and cut into 1/4-inch pieces

2 garlic cloves, crushed with garlic press

1 jalapeño chile, seeded and minced

3 limes

12 ounces red potatoes, unpeeled and cut into 1/4-inch pieces

1 can (14 to 14 1/2 ounces) vegetable broth or 1 3/4 cups Vegetable Broth (page 16)

1/2 teaspoon salt

4 cups water

2 cups corn kernels cut from cobs (3 to 4 ears)

1 cup loosely packed fresh cilantro, chopped

1 ripe avocado, cut into 1/4-inch pieces

plain tortilla chips, coarsely broken (optional)

1. In nonstick 5- to 6-quart saucepot or Dutch oven, heat oil over medium-high heat until hot. Add onion, carrots, garlic, and jalapeño and cook, stirring occasionally, until vegetables are golden, about 15 minutes.

2. Meanwhile, from limes, grate 1/2 teaspoon peel and squeeze 1/3 cup juice; set aside.

3. Add potatoes, broth, salt, and water to saucepot; heat to boiling over medium-high heat. Reduce heat to low; cover and simmer 5 minutes. Add corn; cover and simmer until potatoes are tender, about 5 minutes.

4. Stir in cilantro, lime peel, and lime juice. Top each serving with avocado, then sprinkle with tortilla chips, if you like.

Each serving: About 350 calories, 8g protein, 58g carbohydrate, 14g total fat (2g saturated), 0mg cholesterol, 945mg sodium.

Tomato Soup

A tasty way to use up every last ripe tomato. For a creamier version, stir in heavy or light cream or plain yogurt to taste.

PREP: 20 MINUTES   COOK: 1 HOUR 10 MINUTES
MAKES ABOUT 8 CUPS OR 8 FIRST-COURSE SERVINGS

1 tablespoon butter or margarine
1 medium onion, finely chopped
1 stalk celery, finely chopped
1 carrot, peeled and finely chopped
1 garlic clove, crushed with garlic press
2 teaspoons fresh thyme leaves
4 pounds ripe tomatoes, cut into pieces

1 can (14 to 14 1/2 ounces) chicken broth or 1 3/4 cups Chicken Broth (page 74)
3/4 teaspoon salt
1/4 teaspoon coarsely ground black pepper
1 bay leaf
1/2 cup water
snipped chives (optional)

1. In 5-quart Dutch oven, melt butter over low heat. Add onion, celery, and carrot; cook until tender, about 10 minutes. Stir in garlic and thyme; cook 1 minute.

2. Add tomatoes, broth, salt, pepper, bay leaf, and water; heat to boiling over high heat. Reduce heat to medium-low and simmer, uncovered, until tomatoes have broken up and mixture has thickened slightly, about 45 minutes. Discard bay leaf.

3. Spoon one-third of mixture into blender; cover, with center part of lid removed, and puree until smooth. Pour into large bowl. Repeat twice more with remaining mixture.

4. Refrigerate soup to serve cold, or clean Dutch oven and reheat soup to serve hot. Sprinkle with chives, if you like.

Each serving: About 80 calories, 3g protein, 13g carbohydrate, 3g total fat (2g saturated), 4mg cholesterol, 405mg sodium.

Tomato and Rice Soup

Tomato and Rice Soup

Old-fashioned comfort food with a whole-grain twist. If you can't find either Wehani (an aromatic, reddish-brown rice that splits slightly when cooked and has a chewy texture) or black Japonica (a dark rice that tastes like a cross between basmati and wild rice), you can use long-grain brown rice.

PREP: 20 MINUTES   COOK: 50 MINUTES
MAKES ABOUT 7½ CUPS, 8 FIRST-COURSE, OR 4 MAIN-DISH SERVINGS

1/2 cup Wehani, black Japonica, or long-grain brown rice
1 tablespoon butter or margarine
1 medium onion, finely chopped
1 stalk celery, finely chopped
1 carrot, peeled and finely chopped
1 garlic clove, crushed with garlic press
1/4 teaspoon dried thyme
1 can (28 ounces) plum tomatoes

1 can (14 to 14½ ounces) chicken broth or 1¾ cups Chicken Broth (page 74)
1/2 teaspoon salt
1/4 teaspoon coarsely ground black pepper
1 bay leaf
1/2 cup loosely packed fresh parsley, chopped

1. Prepare rice as label directs but do not add salt, butter, or margarine; set rice aside.

2. Meanwhile, in 4-quart saucepan, melt butter over medium heat. Add onion, celery, carrot; cook, stirring occasionally, until tender, about 10 minutes. Stir in garlic and thyme; cook 1 minute.

3. Add tomatoes with their juice, broth, salt, pepper, bay leaf, and water; heat to boiling over high heat, breaking up tomatoes with side of spoon. Reduce heat to medium-low and cook, covered, 30 minutes. Discard bay leaf.

4. Spoon half of mixture into blender; cover, with center part of lid removed to let steam escape, and puree until almost smooth. Pour into large bowl. Repeat with remaining mixture. Return puree to saucepan; heat over high heat until hot. Remove from heat; add cooked rice and chopped parsley.

Each first-course serving: About 95 calories, 3g protein, 16g carbohydrate, 2g total fat (1g saturated), 4mg cholesterol, 480mg sodium.

Tuscan Pappa al Pomodoro

The bread acts as the thickener for this comforting Italian tomato soup. It's a cinch to prepare!

PREP: 35 MINUTES PLUS STANDING   COOK: 15 MINUTES
MAKES ABOUT 10 CUPS OR 10 FIRST-COURSE SERVINGS

1 loaf (8 ounces) several-days-old Tuscan or other country-style bread
3^1/$_2$ pounds ripe tomatoes
4 garlic cloves, minced
1 teaspoon salt
^{1}/$_2$ cup extravirgin olive oil
^{1}/$_2$ teaspoon coarsely ground black pepper

1 can (14 to 14^1/$_2$ ounces) chicken or vegetable broth, or 1^3/$_4$ cups Chicken Broth (page 74) or Vegetable Broth (page 16)
3 cups water
^{1}/$_3$ cup minced fresh parsley
^{1}/$_3$ cup thinly sliced fresh basil

1. Cut bread into 1-inch cubes; place on wire rack to dry, about 1 hour.
2. Meanwhile, peel, seed, and chop tomatoes; set aside. On cutting board, with side of chef's knife, mash garlic with salt to form a smooth paste.
3. In 5-quart Dutch oven, heat oil over low heat. Add garlic paste and cook, stirring, 2 minutes. Stir in bread cubes and pepper and cook, stirring, 2 minutes. Add tomatoes and cook, stirring, 2 minutes longer.
4. Stir in broth and water; heat to boiling over high heat. Remove from heat; cover and let stand 1 hour.
5. To serve, stir or whisk vigorously until bread has broken up and mixture is almost smooth. Serve soup warm or reheat to serve hot. Just before serving, stir in parsley and basil.

Each serving: About 200 calories, 4g protein, 19g carbohydrate, 12g total fat (2g saturated), 0mg cholesterol, 495mg sodium.

Thai Coconut Soup

A quick, exotic and delicious soup, full of protein and flavor.

PREP: 15 MINUTES   COOK: 5 MINUTES
MAKES ABOUT 9 CUPS OR 4 MAIN-DISH SERVINGS

2 small carrots, each cut crosswise in half

1/2 medium red pepper

1 can (14 ounces) light unsweetened coconut milk (not cream of coconut), well stirred

2 garlic cloves, crushed with garlic press

1 piece (2 inches) peeled fresh ginger, cut into 4 slices

1/2 teaspoon ground coriander

1/2 teaspoon ground cumin

1/4 teaspoon ground red pepper (cayenne)

12 ounces firm tofu, cut into 1-inch pieces

2 cans (14 to 14 1/2 ounces each) vegetable broth or chicken broth or 3 1/2 cups Chicken Broth (page 74) or Vegetable Broth (page 16)

1 tablespoon Asian fish sauce

1 tablespoon fresh lime juice

1 cup water

2 green onions, sliced

1/2 cup chopped fresh cilantro

1. With vegetable peeler, remove lengthwise strips from carrots and edge of red pepper. Set aside.

2. In 5-quart Dutch oven, heat 1/2 cup coconut milk to boiling over medium heat. Add garlic, ginger, coriander, cumin, and ground red pepper, and cook, stirring, 1 minute.

3. Increase heat to medium-high. Stir in tofu, broth, carrot strips, pepper strips, fish sauce, lime juice, water, and remaining coconut milk; heat just to simmering. Remove and discard ginger. Stir in green onions and cilantro just before serving.

Each serving: About 210 calories, 11g protein, 14g carbohydrate, 17g total fat (6g saturated), 0mg cholesterol, 1,060mg sodium.

Creamy Asparagus Soup

A classic to celebrate spring—asparagus is at its peak in May. Buy it on the day you plan to cook it or, at most, a day ahead. This soup is delicious served with crispy bread sticks.

PREP: 10 MINUTES   COOK: ABOUT 25 MINUTES

MAKES 5 1/2 CUPS OR 4 FIRST-COURSE SERVINGS

1 tablespoon butter or margarine
1 small onion, coarsely chopped
1 1/2 pounds asparagus, trimmed and coarsely chopped
1 can (14 to 14 1/2 ounces) chicken broth or vegetable broth or 1 3/4 cups Chicken Broth (page 74) or Vegetable Broth (page 16)

1/2 teaspoon salt
1/8 teaspoon ground black pepper
1 cup water
1/4 cup heavy or whipping cream
sliced green onions and steamed thin asparagus spears (optional)

1. In 4-quart saucepan, melt butter over medium heat. Add onion and cook, stirring often, until tender and lightly golden, 8 to 10 minutes. Add asparagus and cook, stirring occasionally, 5 minutes.

2. Add broth, salt, pepper, and water; heat to boiling over high heat. Reduce heat to low; cover and simmer until asparagus is very tender, 8 to 10 minutes. Remove from heat.

3. Spoon half of mixture into blender; cover, with center part of lid removed to let steam escape, and puree until very smooth. Pour into large bowl. Repeat with remaining mixture. (Or, if you like, use hand blender, following manufacturer's directions.)

4. Clean saucepan and return puree to pan. Stir in cream and heat through over low heat (do not boil). To serve, top with green onions and asparagus spears, if you like.

Each serving: About 125 calories, 4g protein, 5g carbohydrate, 10g total fat (5g saturated), 26mg cholesterol, 779mg sodium.

Creamy Asparagus Soup

Creamy Corn Chowder

It's made with a hint of smoky bacon and spicy jalapeño. We simmered the corncobs with the broth for a more intense corn flavor.

PREP: 25 MINUTES   COOK: 40 MINUTES

MAKES ABOUT 9 1/2 CUPS OR 8 FIRST-COURSE OR 4 MAIN-DISH SERVINGS

6 medium ears corn, husks and silk removed
4 slices bacon, cut into 1/2-inch pieces
1 medium red onion, finely chopped
1 jalapeño chile, seeded and minced
1 garlic clove, minced
2 tablespoons all-purpose flour
1/2 teaspoon salt
1/8 teaspoon ground black pepper

2 cans (14 to 14 1/2 ounces each) chicken broth or 3 1/2 cups Chicken Broth (page 74)
2 cups half-and-half or light cream
1 pound red potatoes (6 medium), cut into 1/2-inch pieces
2 small ripe tomatoes (8 ounces), peeled, seeded, and chopped
thinly sliced basil leaves

1. Cut kernels from corncobs (about 3 cups). Reserve 3 corncobs, discarding the rest.

2. In 5-quart Dutch oven, cook bacon over medium heat until browned. With slotted spoon, transfer bacon to paper towels to drain.

3. To bacon drippings in Dutch oven, add onion and jalapeño and cook, stirring, over low heat until tender but not browned, about 6 to 8 minutes. Add garlic; cook 1 minute. Stir in flour, salt, and pepper; cook, stirring, 1 minute.

4. Stir in broth, half-and-half, potatoes, and reserved corncobs; heat to boiling over high heat. Reduce heat to low; cover and simmer until potatoes are fork-tender, 10 to 15 minutes.

5. Discard corncobs; stir in corn kernels and heat through. Transfer chowder to warm tureen. Stir in tomatoes and bacon; sprinkle with basil.

Each first-course serving: About 275 calories, 9g protein, 31g carbohydrate, 14g total fat (7g saturated), 27mg cholesterol, 570mg sodium.

Creamy Corn Bisque

Neither your family nor your dinner guests would believe that you prepared this hearty yet elegant starter in less than fifteen minutes—with the help of some canned and frozen products. But you don't have to tell them.

PREP: 3 MINUTES   COOK: ABOUT 10 MINUTES

MAKES ABOUT 8 CUPS OR 8 FIRST-COURSE SERVINGS

1 can (14 3/4 ounces) creamed-style corn
1 can (14 to 14 1/2 ounces) chicken broth or 1 3/4 cups Chicken Broth (page 74)
1 can (10 3/4 ounces) condensed cream of potato soup
1 package (10 ounces) frozen whole-kernel corn

3 cups whole milk
2 green onions, trimmed and thinly sliced
1/8 teaspoon ground red pepper (cayenne)
4 slices fully cooked bacon, crumbled

1. In 4-quart saucepan, heat creamed-style corn, broth, potato soup, frozen corn, milk, green onions, and ground red pepper to boiling over high heat, stirring occasionally.

2. To serve, garnish soup with crumbled bacon.

Each serving: About 175 calories, 7g protein, 25g carbohydrate, 6g total fat (3g saturated), 17mg cholesterol, 770mg sodium.

Quickie Cream
of Vegetable Soups

Start with a package of the frozen vegetable of your choice, a can of broth, and seasonings; in twenty-five minutes you'll have a luscious, creamy, lower-fat soup.

PREP: 5 MINUTES   COOK: 20 MINUTES

MAKES ABOUT 3 3/4 CUPS OR 4 FIRST-COURSE SERVINGS

1 tablespoon butter or margarine	1/4 teaspoon dried thyme
1 medium onion, finely chopped	1/8 teaspoon salt
1 can (14 to 14 1/2 ounces) chicken broth or 1 3/4 cups Chicken Broth (page 74)	1/8 teaspoon ground black pepper
	1 1/2 cups milk
	2 teaspoons fresh lemon juice
1 package (10 ounces) frozen vegetable (see table)	optional garnish (see chart, opposite)

1. In 2-quart saucepan, melt butter over medium heat. Stir in onion and cook, stirring occasionally, until tender, about 5 minutes. Add broth, frozen vegetable, thyme, salt, and pepper; heat to boiling over high heat. Reduce heat to low and simmer, uncovered, 10 minutes.

2. Spoon half of mixture into blender; cover, with center part of lid removed to let steam escape, and puree until smooth. Pour into large bowl. Repeat with remaining mixture.

3. Return puree to same clean saucepan; stir in milk. Heat through over medium heat, stirring often (do not boil, or soup may curdle). Remove from heat; stir in lemon juice. Garnish, if you like.

Each serving corn, lima bean, or pea soup: About 170 calories, 9g protein, 20g carbohydrate, 7g total fat (4g saturated), 18mg cholesterol, 509mg sodium.

Each serving asparagus, cauliflower, kale, or squash soup: About 130 calories, 8g protein, 11g carbohydrate, 7g total fat (4g saturated), 18mg cholesterol, 474mg sodium.

TYPE OF VEGETABLE	EXTRA INGREDIENT	ADDITIONAL COOKING STEPS	OPTIONAL GARNISH
asparagus	$1/4$ tsp. dried tarragon	none	snipped fresh chives
cauliflower flowerets	$1/2$ tsp. curry powder	Add curry after cooking onion; cook 30 seconds.	chopped fresh apple
chopped kale	1 garlic clove, minced	Add garlic after cooking onion; cook 30 seconds. Add milk to kale mixture before pureeing.	crumbled cooked bacon
lima beans	none	none	chopped fresh thyme
peas	$1/4$ tsp. dried mint	none	swirl of sour cream
whole-kernel corn	$3/4$ tsp. chili powder	Add chili powder after cooking onion; cook 30 seconds.	chopped fresh cilantro
winter squash	$1/4$ tsp. pumpkin-pie spice	Add spice after cooking onion; cook 30 seconds.	chopped tomato

Yellow Squash and Basil Soup

Yellow Squash and Basil Soup

For decoration, float a bright edible flower, such as a pansy or nasturtium, on top of the soup or place it on the rim of the bowl.

PREP: 10 MINUTES   COOK: 30 MINUTES

MAKES 8 CUPS OR 10 FIRST-COURSE SERVINGS

4 tablespoons butter or margarine

1 medium onion, finely chopped

4 small yellow squashes (about 8 ounces each), trimmed and sliced

3 carrots (1/2 pound), peeled and sliced

1 can (14 to 141/2 ounces) chicken broth or 13/4 cups Chicken Broth (page 74)

11/2 cups water

1/2 cup half-and-half or light cream

11/4 teaspoons salt

1/4 teaspoon coarsely ground black pepper

1 cup loosely packed fresh basil, chopped

1. In 4-quart saucepan, melt butter over medium heat. Add onion and cook, stirring frequently, until onion is tender but not brown, about 8 minutes.

2. Add squash and carrots and stir to coat with onion mixture. Add broth and water; heat to boiling over high heat. Reduce heat to low, cover and simmer until vegetables are tender, about 20 minutes.

3. Spoon half of mixture into blender; cover, with center part of lid removed to let steam escape, and puree until smooth. Pour into large bowl. Repeat with remaining mixture.

4. Return puree to same clean saucepan. Stir in half-and-half, salt, and pepper; heat through. Stir in chopped basil just before serving.

Each serving: About 55 calories, 3g protein, 9g carbohydrate, 2g total fat (3g saturated), 16mg cholesterol, 831mg sodium.

Chestnut and Apple Soup

An elegant and festive addition to any holiday supper.

PREP: 1 HOUR 15 MINUTES   COOK: 45 MINUTES
MAKES ABOUT 9 CUPS OR 10 FIRST-COURSE SERVINGS

1 pound fresh chestnuts (or 30 shelled, cooked, whole chestnuts packed in water, drained)
2 tablespoons butter or margarine
1 medium onion, chopped
1 large carrot, chopped
4 Granny Smith apples (about 1 1/2 pounds), peeled, cored, and coarsely chopped
1 can (14 to 14 1/2 ounces) chicken broth, or 1 3/4 cups Chicken Broth (page 74)

2 tablespoons light brown sugar
1 tablespoon fresh thyme, or 1 teaspoon dried thyme
3/4 teaspoon salt
1/4 teaspoon freshly ground black pepper
1 cinnamon stick (3 inches)
3 cups water
1 cup heavy or whipping cream
cooked crumbled chestnuts and thin apple slices for garnish

1. Prepare chestnuts: In 4-quart saucepan, heat chestnuts and enough *water* to cover to boiling over high heat. Reduce heat to medium and cook 10 minutes. Remove saucepan from heat. With slotted spoon, transfer 3 or 4 chestnuts at a time to cutting board; cool slightly. Cut each chestnut in half. With tip of small knife, scrape out chestnut meat from shell (skin will stay in shell). Set aside.

2. In nonreactive 5-quart saucepot, heat butter over medium heat until melted. Add onion and carrot and cook, stirring occasionally, until vegetables are tender, 7 to 8 minutes. Add chestnuts and apples and cook until apples soften, about 5 minutes. Stir in broth, sugar, thyme, salt, pepper, cinnamon stick, and water; heat to boiling over high heat. Reduce heat to low; cover and simmer 20 minutes. Remove and discard cinnamon.

3. Spoon one-third of hot soup into blender; cover with center part of lid removed to let steam escape, and puree until smooth. Pour soup into bowl. Repeat with remaining mixture.

4. Return pureed soup to saucepot. Stir in cream; heat through. Garnish each serving with crumbled chestnuts and apple slices.

Each serving: About 205 calories, 2g protein, 4g carbohydrate, 12g total fat (6g saturated), 33mg cholesterol, 400mg sodium.

Chestnut and Apple Soup

Herbed Winter Squash Soup

It's hard to believe that a soup as tasty as this one could be so quick and easy to prepare: using frozen pureed squash is the key.

PREP: 5 MINUTES   COOK: 20 MINUTES
MAKES 8 CUPS OR 8 FIRST-COURSE SERVINGS

2 packages (10 to 12 ounces each) frozen pureed butternut or winter squash
2 cans (14 to 14 1/2 ounces each) chicken broth or 3 1/2 cups Chicken Broth (page 74)
1 jar (16 ounces) unsweetened applesauce

1 tablespoon crushed fresh thyme
1/2 teaspoon salt
1/4 teaspoon coarsely ground pepper
1 cup water
8 thyme sprigs

In 4-quart saucepan, combine squash, broth, applesauce, thyme, salt, pepper, and water; heat to boiling over medium-high heat. Reduce heat; cover and simmer 15 minutes. Garnish with thyme sprigs.

Each serving: About 85 calories, 2g protein, 19g carbohydrate, 1g total fat (0g saturated), 0mg cholesterol, 560mg sodium.

Quick Tip: Making Short Work of Butternut Squash

Butternut squash comes in such an awkward shape. Is there an easy way to peel and cut it?

Shaped like a bowling pin, butternut squash can be a difficult vegetable to slice and dice until you get the hang of it. First, use a chef's knife to cut off the top and bottom ends of the squash. Then cut the squash in two, at the point that the narrow part (neck) meets the rounded bottom. Cut the bottom in half and, with a spoon, scoop out the seeds from both halves. Using a sharp, swivel-blade Y-shaped vegetable peeler, remove the peel from the two bottom halves and the neck. No peeler? Place the bottom halves cut side down; cut into 1 1/2- to 2-inch-wide slices, then cut away the tough skin from each slice. Repeat with the neck of the squash. Finally, dice, slice, or cut the squash flesh into chunks, as recipe directs. (Some squashes, such as acorn and Hubbard, can be even more difficult to peel. Simply cut into pieces and bake or roast with the skin on.)

Curried Butternut Squash Soup

The secret to making this low-fat soup thick and velvety smooth without a drop of cream is using a blender to puree the soup in small batches. It freezes very well: reheat the soup directly from its frozen state when ready to serve.

PREP: 20 MINUTES   COOK: 40 MINUTES
MAKES 12 CUPS OR 12 FIRST-COURSE SERVINGS

3 tablespoons butter or margarine
2 large onions (12 ounces each), sliced
1 tablespoon curry powder
2 large butternut squashes (3 1/2 pounds total), peeled, seeded, and cut into 1/2-inch pieces

2 cans (14 to 14 1/2 ounces each) chicken broth or 3 1/2 cups Chicken Broth (page 74)
1/2 teaspoon salt
2 1/4 cups water

1. In 5-quart Dutch oven or saucepot, melt 2 tablespoons butter over medium heat. Add onions and cook, stirring occasionally, until golden and tender, 18 to 20 minutes. Add curry and remaining 1 tablespoon butter and cook, stirring, 1 minute.

2. Add squash, broth, salt, and water; heat to boiling. Reduce heat to low; cover and simmer soup until squash is very tender, about 20 minutes.

3. Spoon one-third of mixture into blender; cover, with center part of lid removed to let steam escape, and puree until very smooth. Pour into large bowl. Repeat twice more with remaining mixture.

4. Clean Dutch oven and return soup to pan; heat through.

Each serving: About 95 calories, 3g protein, 15g carbohydrate, 3g total fat (2g saturated), 8mg cholesterol, 351mg sodium.

Butternut Squash Soup with Parsnips and Apples

The subtle sweetness of parsnips and the tartness of Granny Smith apples give this squash soup a pleasingly complex flavor.

PREP: 30 MINUTES   COOK: ABOUT 25 MINUTES
MAKES ABOUT 12 CUPS OR 12 FIRST-COURSE SERVINGS

2 tablespoons butter or margarine
2 large shallots (about 4 ounces), finely chopped ($1/2$ cup)
2 stalks celery, finely chopped
3 pounds butternut squash (about 2 medium), peeled, seeded, and cut into 1-inch pieces
1 pound parsnips, peeled and cut into 1-inch pieces
1 pound Granny Smith apples (about 3 medium), peeled, cored, and cut into 1-inch pieces

2 teaspoons chopped fresh thyme
1 teaspoon salt
$1/4$ teaspoon coarsely ground black pepper
4 cans (14 to $14 1/2$ ounces each) chicken broth or 7 cups Chicken Broth (page 74)
plain low-fat yogurt

1. In $5 1/2$- to 6-quart Dutch oven, melt butter over medium heat. Add shallots and celery; cover and cook, stirring occasionally, until softened, about 5 minutes. Stir in squash, parsnips, apples, thyme, salt, and pepper. Add 2 cans broth; cover and heat to boiling over high heat. Reduce heat to low and simmer, covered, until vegetables are very tender, about 20 minutes.

2. Spoon one-third of mixture into blender; cover, with center part of lid removed to let steam escape, and puree until smooth. Pour into large bowl. Repeat twice more with remaining mixture.

3. Clean Dutch oven and return soup to pan. Stir in remaining 2 cans broth; heat over medium heat until heated through. Garnish each serving with a swirl of yogurt.

Each serving: About 120 calories, 3g protein, 22g carbohydrate, 3g total fat (2g saturated), 5mg cholesterol, 809mg sodium.

Butternut Squash Soup with Parsnips and Apples

Pumpkin-Potato Soup

This lightly spiced seasonal soup is a sure-fire hit at any Thanksgiving dinner!

PREP: 25 MINUTES   COOK: ABOUT 45 MINUTES

MAKES ABOUT 12 CUPS OR 12 FIRST-COURSE SERVINGS

2 tablespoons olive oil

1 large onion (12 ounces), coarsely chopped

3 garlic cloves, minced

1 1/2 teaspoons ground cumin

1 1/2 teaspoons ground coriander

1/8 teaspoon ground red pepper (cayenne)

1 can (29 ounces) solid-pack pumpkin (not pumpkin-pie mix)

1 can (14 to 14 1/2 ounces) chicken broth or 1 3/4 cups Chicken Broth (page 74)

1 large all-purpose potato (8 ounces), peeled and cut into 1-inch pieces

1 tablespoon sugar

1 1/2 teaspoons salt

1/8 teaspoon coarsely ground black pepper

6 cups water

plain low-fat yogurt and toasted pumpkin seeds (optional)

1. In 6-quart saucepan, heat oil over medium heat until hot. Add onion and cook, stirring occasionally, until tender and golden, about 20 minutes.
2. Add garlic, cumin, coriander, and ground red pepper and cook, stirring, 1 minute. Stir in pumpkin, broth, potato, sugar, salt, black pepper, and water; heat to boiling over high heat. Reduce heat to medium-low; cover and simmer until potato is fork-tender, about 20 minutes.
3. Remove saucepan from heat. Following manufacturer's directions, use electric hand blender to puree pumpkin mixture in saucepan until very smooth. (Or, spoon one-third of mixture into blender; cover, with center part of lid removed to let steam escape, and puree mixture until very smooth. Pour into large bowl. Repeat twice more with remaining mixture.)

4. Clean saucepan and return soup to pan. Reheat over medium heat until hot. Serve with yogurt and pumpkin seeds, if you like.

Each serving: About 75 calories, 2g protein, 12g carbohydrate, 3g total fat (1g saturated), 0mg cholesterol, 440mg sodium.

Do-ahead tip: If not serving the soup right away, cool it slightly, then transfer it to airtight containers and refrigerate up to 3 days. Reheat in a saucepot over medium heat, stirring occasionally.

Spiced Pumpkin Soup

Spiced Pumpkin Soup

Be sure to use 100-percent pure pumpkin, not filling mix for pumpkin pie, which comes already spiced. It will not produce the right flavor.

PREP: 5 MINUTES   COOK: ABOUT 30 MINUTES
MAKES 9 1/2 CUPS OR 8 FIRST-COURSE SERVINGS

2 tablespoons butter or margarine
1 carrot, peeled and finely chopped
1 medium onion, finely chopped
2 small garlic cloves, minced
2 teaspoons ground cumin
1/2 teaspoon ground cinnamon
1 carton (32 ounces) chicken or vegetable broth or 4 cups Chicken Broth (page 74) or Vegetable Broth (page 16)

1 can (29 ounces) solid-pack pumpkin (not pumpkin-pie mix)
1 can or bottle (12 to 15.2 ounces) carrot juice
1/2 cup roasted shelled pumpkin seeds (pepitas)

1. In 4-quart saucepan, melt butter over medium heat. Add carrot and onion and cook, stirring frequently, until soft, 8 to 10 minutes. Add garlic, cumin, and cinnamon, and cook, stirring, 1 minute.

2. Add broth, pumpkin, and carrot juice; stir to combine. Cover and heat to boiling over high heat. Reduce heat to low; simmer, covered, 15 minutes.

3. Stir soup just before serving. Pass pumpkin seeds to sprinkle over soup.

Each serving: About 190 calories, 8g protein, 19g carbohydrate, 10g total fat (3g saturated), 8mg cholesterol, 552mg sodium.

Tip: If you can't find roasted pumpkin seeds in your supermarket, roast them yourself: In dry 10-inch skillet, toast pumpkin seeds over medium heat until lightly browned.

Potato and Chive Soup

A delicious and creamy soup made with yellow potatoes, vegetables, and chicken broth—but not a drop of cream.

PREP: 15 MINUTES   COOK: ABOUT 30 MINUTES

MAKES ABOUT 6 CUPS OR 6 FIRST-COURSE OR 4 MAIN-DISH SERVINGS

2 tablespoons butter or margarine
1 medium onion, chopped
1 medium stalk celery, chopped
1 medium carrot, peeled and chopped
2 garlic cloves, minced
1 1/2 pounds yellow potatoes, peeled
   and cut into 1/2-inch pieces
1 can (14 to 14 1/2 ounces) chicken
   broth or 1 3/4 cups Chicken Broth
   (page 74)

3/4 teaspoon salt
1/4 teaspoon coarsely ground black
   pepper
3 cups water
1/4 cup snipped fresh chives

1. In 4-quart saucepan, melt butter over medium heat. Add onion, celery, and carrot and cook, stirring occasionally, until vegetables are tender, about 10 minutes. Add garlic; cook, stirring, 1 minute. Add potatoes, broth, salt, pepper, and water; heat to boiling over high heat. Reduce heat to low; simmer, uncovered, until potatoes are tender, about 15 minutes. Remove saucepan from heat.

2. Spoon half of mixture into blender; cover, with center part of lid removed to let steam escape, and puree until smooth. Pour into large bowl. Repeat with remaining mixture. (If you like, use a hand blender, following manufacturer's directions, to puree mixture in saucepan.)

3. Return soup to same clean saucepan and heat through over medium heat, stirring occasionally. Remove from heat. Stir in chives.

Each first-course serving: About 135 calories, 3g protein, 22g carbohydrate, 5g total fat (4g saturated), 16mg cholesterol, 622mg sodium.

Chunky Vegetable Chowder

An assortment of your favorite fall vegetables makes this hearty soup a tasty and healthful comfort food.

PREP: 30 MINUTES   COOK: ABOUT 30 MINUTES

MAKES ABOUT 13 CUPS OR 6 MAIN-DISH SERVINGS

2 tablespoons olive oil
1 jumbo onion (1 pound), cut into
   1/4-inch pieces
12 ounces red potatoes, unpeeled
   and cut into 1/2-inch pieces
3 carrots (8 ounces), peeled and cut
   into 1/4-inch pieces
2 parsnips (about 8 ounces), peeled
   and cut into 1/4-inch pieces
2 stalks celery, cut into 1/4-inch
   pieces
2 garlic cloves, crushed with garlic
   press

1 can (14 to 14 1/2 ounces)
   vegetable broth or 1 3/4 cups
   Vegetable Broth (page 16)
3/4 teaspoon salt
1/4 teaspoon dried thyme
4 1/2 cups water
1 package (10 ounces) frozen
   Fordhook lima beans
12 ounces escarole or Swiss chard,
   tough stems trimmed and leaves
   coarsely chopped

1. In nonstick 5- to 6-quart saucepot or Dutch oven, heat oil over medium-high heat until very hot. Add onion, potatoes, carrots, parsnips, celery, and garlic and cook, stirring occasionally, until vegetables are lightly browned, about 15 minutes.

2. Add broth, salt, thyme, and water; heat to boiling over medium-high heat. Stir in lima beans and escarole; heat to boiling. Reduce heat to low; cover and simmer until vegetables are tender, 10 minutes.

Each serving: About 220 calories, 7g protein, 39g carbohydrate, 5g total fat (1g saturated), 0mg cholesterol, 675mg sodium.

Barley Minestrone

Top this soup with a dollop of our homemade pesto, which you can make in a mini food processor. No mini processor? Store-bought refrigerated pesto makes an excellent stand-in—although it's not as light as our version.

PREP: ABOUT 25 MINUTES   COOK: ABOUT 50 MINUTES
MAKES ABOUT 10 1/2 CUPS OR 6 MAIN-DISH SERVINGS

1 cup pearl barley
1 tablespoon olive oil
2 cups thinly sliced green cabbage (about 1/4 small head)
2 large carrots, each cut lengthwise in half, then crosswise into 1/2-inch-thick slices
2 large stalks celery, cut into 1/2-inch dice
1 medium onion, cut into 1/2-inch dice
1 garlic clove, finely chopped

3 cups water
2 cans (14 to 14 1/2 ounces each) vegetable broth or 3 1/2 cups Vegetable Broth (page 16)
1 can (14 to 14 1/2 ounces) diced tomatoes
Salt
1 medium zucchini (about 6 ounces), cut into 1/2-inch dice
1/4 pound green beans, cut into 1/2-inch pieces (about 1 cup)

1. Heat 5- to 6-quart Dutch oven over medium-high heat until hot. Add barley and cook 3 to 4 minutes or until toasted and fragrant, stirring constantly. Transfer barley to small bowl; set aside.

2. In same Dutch oven, heat oil over medium-high heat until hot. Add cabbage, carrots, celery, and onion; cook 8 to 10 minutes or until vegetables are tender and lightly browned, stirring occasionally. Add garlic and cook 30 seconds or until fragrant. Stir in barley, water, broth, tomatoes, and 1/4 teaspoon salt. Cover and heat to boiling over high heat. Reduce heat to low and simmer, covered, 25 minutes.

3. Stir zucchini and beans into barley mixture; increase heat to medium and cook, covered, 10 to 15 minutes longer until all vegetables and barley are tender.

4. Ladle minestrone into 6 large soup bowls. Top each serving with some pesto.

Each serving soup without pesto: About 215 calories, 7g protein, 42g carbohydrate, 4g total fat (0g saturated), 9g fiber, 0mg cholesterol, 690mg sodium.

Light Pesto

1 cup firmly packed fresh basil
2 tablespoons olive oil
2 tablespoons water
Salt

¹/₄ cup freshly grated Parmesan or
  Pecorino Romano cheese
1 garlic clove, finely chopped

In a blender container with narrow base, or in mini food processor, combine basil, oil, water, and ¹/₄ teaspoon salt; cover and blend until mixture is pureed. Transfer pesto to small bowl; stir in Parmesan and garlic. Makes about ¹/₂ cup.

Each teaspoon pesto: About 15 calories, 0g protein, 0g carbohydrate, 1g total fat (0g saturated) 0g fiber, 1mg cholesterol, 35mg sodium.

Barley Minestrone with Light Pesto

Chunky Tomato Soup with Tofu-Parmesan Croutons

With tofu as an added source of lean protein, this soup is packed with vitamins for a super-healthy lunch or light dinner.

PREP: 15 MINUTES   COOK/BROIL: ABOUT 30 MINUTES
MAKES ABOUT 6 1/2 CUPS OR 4 MAIN-DISH SERVINGS

1 tablespoon olive oil
1 cup packaged shredded carrots
1 small onion, finely chopped
2 garlic cloves, crushed with press

2 cans (28 ounces each) whole
  tomatoes in juice
1 cup water
Salt and ground black pepper

1. In 6-quart saucepan, heat oil over medium-high heat. Add carrots, onion, and garlic, and cook, covered, 5 to 7 minutes or until vegetables begin to brown, stirring occasionally.

2. Stir in tomatoes with their juice, water, 1/2 teaspoon salt, and 1/4 teaspoon pepper, breaking up tomatoes with spoon; heat to boiling. Reduce heat to medium-low; partially cover and simmer 20 minutes.

3. To serve, with potato masher, crush tomatoes in soup. Top each serving of soup with 2 croutons.

Each serving (with croutons); About 270 calories, 16g protein, 31g carbohydrate, 12g total fat (3g saturated), 6g fiber, 7mg cholesterol, 1,125mg sodium.

Tofu-Parmesan Croutons

1 package (14 ounces) firm tofu,
  drained
1 slice whole wheat bread, coarsely
  grated into crumbs

1/3 cup freshly grated Parmesan or
  Pecorino Romano cheese

Preheat broiler. Cut tofu into 8 slices. Place slices between layers of paper towels and gently press to extract excess moisture. In bowl, combine crumbs and Parmesan. Spray cookie sheet with nonstick cooking spray. Arrange tofu on cookie sheet; sprinkle with crumb mixture. Place cookie sheet under broiler, 5 to 6 inches from source of heat, and broil tofu 5 to 8 minutes or until browned.

Squash and Black Bean Chili

Fast doesn't have to mean unhealthy. This quick-cooking vegetarian chili is loaded with vitamins, antioxidants, and lean protein.

PREP: 10 MINUTES   COOK: ABOUT 30 MINUTES
MAKES ABOUT 8 CUPS OR 4 MAIN-DISH SERVINGS

1 tablespoon olive oil or canola oil
1 medium yellow pepper, chopped
1 medium onion, chopped
1 medium stalk celery, chopped
2 garlic cloves, crushed with press
2 tablespoons chili powder
2 cans (15 to 19 ounces each) black beans, rinsed and drained
1 package (1¼ pounds) peeled and cut-up butternut squash, cut into 1-inch chunks

1 can (14 to 14½ ounces) fire-roasted diced tomatoes
1 can (14 to 14½ ounces) vegetable broth or 1¾ cups Vegetable Broth (page 16)
Corn tortillas, sour cream, and lime wedges for garnish

1. In 5-quart Dutch oven, heat oil over medium-high heat. Add pepper, onion, and celery, and cook 5 to 8 minutes or just until vegetables are tender, stirring occasionally. Stir in garlic and chili powder and cook 30 seconds or until fragrant, stirring.
2. Meanwhile, in a small bowl, coarsely mash ½ cup beans. Stir all beans, squash, tomatoes, and broth into mixture in Dutch oven; cover and heat to boiling. Reduce heat to low; simmer, covered, 15 minutes or until squash is tender. Serve chili with tortillas, sour cream, and lime if you like.

Each serving: About 315 calories, 15g protein, 67g carbohydrate, 5g total fat (1g saturated), 18g fiber, 0mg cholesterol, 1,200mg sodium.

Sweet-Potato and Peanut Stew

A tasty vegetarian dish with tomatoes, warm spices, and a touch of peanut butter. Microwaving the sweet potatoes helps you finish in a flash.

PREP: 15 MINUTES   COOK: ABOUT 15 MINUTES
MAKES ABOUT 8 CUPS OR 4 MAIN-DISH SERVINGS

3 medium sweet potatoes (about 12 ounces each), well scrubbed and each cut into 1 1/2-inch pieces
1 tablespoon olive oil
2 garlic cloves, crushed with garlic press
1 1/2 teaspoons ground cumin
1/2 teaspoon salt
1/4 teaspoon ground cinnamon
1/8 teaspoon crushed red pepper

2 cans (15 to 19 ounces each) garbanzo beans, rinsed and drained
1 can (14 to 14 1/2 ounces) vegetable broth or 1 3/4 cups Vegetable Broth (page 16)
1 can (14 1/2 ounces) diced tomatoes
1/4 cup creamy peanut butter
1/2 cup loosely packed fresh cilantro, chopped

1. Place potatoes in 2 1/2-quart microwave-safe dish. Cover dish and microwave on High until fork-tender, about 8 minutes.

2. Meanwhile, in 5- to 6-quart saucepot, heat oil over medium-high heat until hot. Add garlic, cumin, salt, cinnamon, and crushed red pepper and cook, stirring, 30 seconds. Stir in beans, broth, tomatoes, and peanut butter until blended and heat to boiling. Cook, stirring occasionally, 1 minute.

3. Reduce heat to medium-low. Add sweet potatoes and simmer, stirring occasionally, 2 to 5 minutes. Stir in cilantro.

Each serving: About 585 calories, 22g protein, 92g carbohydrate, 16g total fat (2g saturated), 0mg cholesterol, 1,725mg sodium.

Sweet-Potato and Peanut Stew

Winter Vegetable Chowder

One of the vegetables in this flavor-packed combo is celery root (also called celeriac), a knobby brown vegetable that tastes like a cross between celery and parsley.

PREP: 20 MINUTES   COOK: ABOUT 7 HOURS

MAKES ABOUT 11 CUPS OR 6 MAIN-DISH SERVINGS

2 medium leeks (about 8 ounces)	2 cans (14 to 14 1/2 ounces each)
3 slices bacon, cut into 1/2-inch	vegetable or chicken broth or 3 1/2
pieces	cups Vegetable Broth (page 16) or
3 large all-purpose potatoes (about	Chicken Broth (page 74)
1 1/2 pounds)	1/2 teaspoon dried thyme
1 large celery root (about 1 1/2	1/2 teaspoon salt
pounds)	1/8 teaspoon ground black pepper
1 medium butternut squash (about	1 cup water
2 1/4 pounds)	1 cup half-and-half or light cream

1. Cut off roots and trim dark green tops from leeks; cut each leek lengthwise in half, then crosswise into 3/4-inch pieces. Rinse leeks in large bowl of cold water, swishing to remove sand. Transfer to colander to drain, leaving sand in bottom of bowl.

2. In 12-inch skillet, cook leeks and bacon over medium-high heat, stirring occasionally, until browned, 7 to 10 minutes.

3. Meanwhile, peel potatoes and cut into 1/2-inch pieces. Trim and peel celery root; cut into 1/2-inch pieces. Trim ends from squash, then cut lengthwise in half; discard seeds. With vegetable peeler, remove peel, then cut squash into 1-inch pieces.

4. Place potatoes, celery root, and squash in 4 1/2- to 6-quart slow cooker. Stir in broth, thyme, salt, pepper, leek mixture, and water. Cover slow cooker and cook on Low setting as manufacturer directs until all vegetables are very tender, 7 to 8 hours.

5. With slotted spoon, transfer about 2 cups cooked vegetables to small bowl. With potato masher, pastry blender, or fork, coarsely mash vegetables. Stir mashed vegetables back into slow cooker, then stir in half-and-half. Heat through on High setting, if necessary.

Each serving: About 380 calories, 9g protein, 55g carbohydrate, 17g total fat (7g saturated), 27mg cholesterol, 1,047mg sodium.

Caldo Verde

In Portugal, this delicious soup gets its rich green color from finely shredded Galician cabbage. Kale, readily available in supermarkets, makes a fine substitute.

PREP: 25 MINUTES   COOK: 35 MINUTES
MAKES ABOUT 10 CUPS OR 5 MAIN-DISH SERVINGS

2 tablespoons olive oil
1 large onion (12 ounces), finely chopped
3 garlic cloves, minced
2 1/2 pounds all-purpose potatoes (about 8 medium), peeled and cut into 2-inch pieces
2 cans (14 to 14 1/2 ounces each) chicken broth or 3 1/2 cups Chicken Broth (page 74)

1 teaspoon salt
1/4 teaspoon coarsely ground black pepper
3 cups water
1 pound kale, tough stems and veins trimmed and leaves very thinly sliced
1/2 cup linguiça or chorizo (optional)

1. In 5-quart Dutch oven, heat oil over medium heat. Add onion and garlic; cook until lightly browned, about 10 minutes.
2. Add potatoes, broth, salt, pepper, and water; heat to boiling over high heat. Reduce heat to low; cover and simmer until potatoes are fork-tender, about 20 minutes.
3. With potato masher, mash potatoes in broth until potatoes are lumpy.
4. Stir in kale; simmer, uncovered, until tender, 5 to 8 minutes. Garnish with the linguiça or chorizo, if you like.

Each serving: About 250 calories, 8g protein, 42g carbohydrate, 7g total fat (1g saturated), 8mg cholesterol, 925mg sodium.

Moroccan Vegetable Stew

A hearty vegetarian stew starring skillet-browned carrots, squash, and onion and sweetened with cinnamon and prunes. Delicious over hot fluffy couscous.

PREP: 15 MINUTES   COOK: ABOUT 40 MINUTES

MAKES ABOUT 6 CUPS OR 4 MAIN-DISH SERVINGS

1 tablespoon olive oil
2 carrots, peeled and cut crosswise into 1/4-inch-thick slices
1 medium butternut squash (about 1 3/4 pounds), peeled, seeded, and cut into 1-inch pieces
1 medium onion, chopped
1 can (15 to 19 ounces) garbanzo beans, rinsed and drained
1 can (14 1/2 ounces) stewed tomatoes
1/2 cup pitted prunes, chopped

1/2 teaspoon ground cinnamon
1/2 teaspoon salt
1/8 to 1/4 teaspoon crushed red pepper
1 1/2 cups water
1 cup couscous (Moroccan pasta)
1/2 can (8 ounces) vegetable or chicken broth or 1 cup Vegetable Broth (page 16) or Chicken Broth (page 74)
2 tablespoons chopped fresh cilantro or parsley

1. In nonstick 12-inch skillet, heat oil over medium-high heat until hot. Add carrots, squash, and onion and cook, stirring occasionally, until golden, about 10 minutes.

2. Stir in beans, tomatoes, prunes, cinnamon, salt, crushed red pepper, and water; heat to boiling. Reduce heat to low; cover and simmer until vegetables are tender, about 30 minutes.

3. Meanwhile, prepare couscous as label directs but use broth in place of water.

4. Stir in cilantro. To serve, spoon stew over couscous.

Each serving: About 485 calories, 16g protein, 94g carbohydrate, 7g total fat (1g saturated), 3mg cholesterol, 1,030mg sodium.

Moroccan Vegetable Stew

New Orleans Green Gumbo

Popular around the Mississippi Delta, this soup has a slightly thickened "gumbo" texture created by the pepper-spiked brown roux and grated potato.

PREP: 40 MINUTES   COOK: 20 MINUTES

MAKES 10 CUPS OR 8 FIRST-COURSE SERVINGS

8 slices bacon, cut into 1/2-inch pieces
1/4 cup all-purpose flour
1 teaspoon salt
1/4 teaspoon ground red pepper (cayenne)
2 cans (14 to 14 1/2 ounces each) chicken broth or 3 1/2 cups Chicken Broth (page 74)

1 1/2 pounds fresh greens (collard or mustard, or a combination), tough stems trimmed and leaves cut into 1/2-inch pieces
1 package (10 ounces) frozen chopped spinach, thawed
1 large all-purpose potato (8 ounces), peeled and grated
4 cups water

1. In 5-quart Dutch oven, cook bacon over medium-low heat until browned. With slotted spoon, transfer to paper towels to drain. Set aside.

2. Discard all but 2 tablespoons bacon drippings from Dutch oven. Stir in flour, salt, and ground red pepper and cook over medium heat, stirring frequently, until golden brown, about 5 minutes.

3. Stir in broth, fresh greens, spinach, potato, and water; heat to boiling over high heat. Reduce heat to low; cover and simmer, stirring occasionally, until soup thickens slightly and greens are tender, 20 to 25 minutes. To serve, sprinkle with bacon.

Each serving: About 145 calories, 7g protein, 14g carbohydrate, 7g total fat (3g saturated), 9mg cholesterol, 735mg sodium.

Tip: Wash and cut greens a day ahead; store, loosely wrapped, in the refrigerator.

Vegetable-Barley Stew

A simple Italian gremolata of parsley, garlic, and lemon tops the stew to add a distinctive tangy element.

PREP: 15 MINUTES   COOK: ABOUT 20 MINUTES
MAKES ABOUT 9 CUPS OR 4 MAIN-DISH SERVINGS

1 cup quick-cooking barley
1 tablespoon olive oil
1 package (20 ounces) peeled and seeded butternut squash, cut into 1/2-inch pieces (4 cups)
2 stalks celery, cut into 1/2-inch pieces
1 medium onion, chopped
1 jar (14 to 16 ounces) marinara sauce
1 package (9 ounces) frozen cut green beans

1/2 can (8 ounces) chicken broth or 1 cup Chicken Broth (page 74)
1/2 teaspoon salt
1/4 teaspoon ground black pepper
1/2 cup loosely packed fresh parsley leaves, chopped
1/2 teaspoon freshly grated lemon peel
1 small garlic clove, minced

1. Cook barley as label directs.
2. Meanwhile, in nonstick 12-inch skillet, heat oil over medium-high heat until hot. Add squash, celery, and onion; cover and cook, stirring occasionally, until lightly browned, about 10 minutes. Stir in marinara sauce, green beans, broth, salt, and pepper. Simmer, uncovered, until slightly thickened, about 4 minutes.
3. In small bowl, with fork, stir parsley, lemon peel, and garlic; set aside.
4. Drain liquid, if any, from barley. Stir barley into vegetables. Sprinkle with parsley mixture to serve.

Each serving: About 320 calories, 9g protein, 60g carbohydrate, 7g total fat (1g saturated), 0mg cholesterol, 985mg sodium.

Curried Vegetable Stew

Curried Vegetable Stew

A fragrant skillet dish flavored with rich Indian spices, raisins, and tomatoes. Serve over rice or with pita bread and plain yogurt.

PREP: 30 MINUTES   COOK: 40 MINUTES

MAKES ABOUT 10 CUPS OR 5 MAIN-DISH SERVINGS

1 tablespoon olive oil
1 medium onion, coarsely chopped
5 cups small cauliflower flowerets (about 1 small head cauliflower)
4 carrots, peeled and each cut lengthwise in half, then crosswise into 1/4-inch-thick slices
1 teaspoon minced, peeled fresh ginger
3 garlic cloves, crushed with garlic press
1 tablespoon curry powder

1 teaspoon ground cumin
3/4 teaspoon salt
1/8 to 1/4 teaspoon ground red pepper (cayenne)
2 cans (15 to 19 ounces each) garbanzo beans, rinsed and drained
1 can (14 to 14 1/2 ounces) diced tomatoes
1/4 cup golden raisins
1/2 cup water
1/2 cup loosely packed fresh cilantro, chopped

1. In nonstick 12-inch skillet, heat oil over medium heat until hot. Add onion and cook, stirring occasionally, 5 minutes. Increase heat to medium-high; add cauliflower and carrots and cook, stirring occasionally, until vegetables are lightly browned, about 10 minutes. Add ginger, garlic, curry powder, cumin, salt, and ground red pepper; cook, stirring, 1 minute.

2. Add garbanzo beans, tomatoes with their juice, raisins, and water; heat to boiling over high heat. Reduce heat to low; cover and simmer until vegetables are tender and sauce has thickened slightly, 15 to 20 minutes. Stir in cilantro.

Each serving: About 430 calories, 18g protein, 74g carbohydrate, 10g total fat (1g saturated), 0mg cholesterol, 1,430mg sodium.

CHICKEN

Spring Ramen Chicken Soup, page 89

Chicken Broth

Nothing beats the flavor of homemade chicken broth. Make it in large batches and freeze in sturdy containers for up to four months. Our recipe has an added bonus: The cooked chicken can be used in casseroles and salads. So rich, it serves as a "base" for many of our other soups and stews.

PREP: 10 MINUTES PLUS COOLING   COOK: 4 HOURS 30 MINUTES
MAKES ABOUT 5 1/2 CUPS

1 chicken (3 to 3 1/2 pounds), including neck (reserve giblets for another use)
2 carrots, peeled and cut into 2-inch pieces
1 stalk celery, cut into 2-inch pieces
1 medium onion, unpeeled and cut into quarters
5 parsley sprigs
1 garlic clove, unpeeled
1/2 teaspoon dried thyme
1/2 bay leaf

1. In 6-quart saucepot, combine chicken, chicken neck, carrots, celery, onion, parsley, garlic, thyme, bay leaf, and *3 quarts water* or enough *water* to cover; heat to boiling over high heat. With slotted spoon, skim foam from surface. Reduce heat to low; cover and simmer, turning chicken once and skimming foam occasionally, 1 hour.
2. Remove from heat; transfer chicken to large bowl. When cool enough to handle, remove skin and bones from chicken. (Reserve chicken meat for another use.) Return skin and bones to Dutch oven and heat to boiling over high heat. Skim foam; reduce heat to low and simmer, uncovered, 3 hours.
3. Strain broth through colander into large bowl; discard solids. Strain again though sieve into containers; cool. Cover and refrigerate to use within 3 days, or freeze up to 4 months.
4. To use, skim and discard fat from surface of broth.

Each cup: About 36 calories, 3g protein, 4g carbohydrate, 1g total fat (1g saturated), 3mg cholesterol, 91mg sodium.

Pressure-Cooker Chicken Broth

In 6-quart pressure cooker, place all ingredients for Chicken Broth but use only *4 cups water.* Following manufacturer's directions, cover pressure cooker and bring up to high pressure (15 pounds). Cook 15 minutes. Remove cooker from heat and allow pressure to drop 5 minutes, then follow manufacturer's directions for quick release of pressure. Strain broth through colander into large bowl; discard solids. Strain again through sieve into containers; cool. Meanwhile, remove skin and bones from chicken; discard. (Reserve chicken for another use.) Cover broth and refrigerate to use within 3 days, or freeze up to 4 months. To use, skim and discard fat from surface of broth.

How to Freeze and Reheat Stews, Soups, Chili, or Sauces

Cool in containers, uncovered, at least 30 minutes in refrigerator or until warm. Cover containers tightly; label and freeze up to 3 months.

When ready to serve, place frozen stew, soup, chili, or sauce, still in covered containers, up to rim in bowl or sink of hot water 1 to 3 minutes or until sides separate from containers. Invert into saucepan or skillet; add $1/4$ to $1/2$ cup water. Cover and heat to boiling over medium heat, stirring occasionally; boil 1 minute, stirring.

Or, invert into microwave-safe bowl or baking dish; cover with waxed paper or vented plastic wrap. Heat in microwave oven on Defrost until most ice crystals are gone and mixture can be easily stirred. Then heat on High until mixture reaches 165°F on instant-read thermometer, stirring gently once during heating.

Basic Chicken Soup

We call this soup "basic," but it is the quintessential comfort food.

PREP: 20 MINUTES PLUS COOLING   COOK: 25 MINUTES
MAKES ABOUT 8½ CUPS OR 4 MAIN-DISH SERVINGS

1 tablespoon olive oil
1 small onion, finely chopped
2 medium carrots, peeled and cut into ¼-inch-thick slices
2 medium stalks celery, cut into ¼-inch-thick slices
2 cans (14 to 14½ ounces each) chicken broth or 3½ cups Chicken Broth (page 74)

⅛ teaspoon ground black pepper
3 cups water
2 skinless, boneless chicken-breast halves (10 ounces)

1. In 4-quart saucepan, heat oil over medium heat until hot. Add onion and cook, stirring occasionally, until tender and lightly browned, about 5 minutes.

2. Add carrots, celery, broth, pepper, and water; heat to boiling over high heat. Add chicken and reduce heat to low; cover and simmer until chicken just loses its pink color throughout and carrots and celery are tender, 8 to 10 minutes.

3. Remove from heat. Using slotted spoon or tongs, transfer chicken to plate; cool slightly. When cool enough to handle, shred chicken into thin strips. Return chicken to soup; heat through.

Each serving: About 150 calories, 20g protein, 7g carbohydrate, 4g total fat (1g saturated), 41mg cholesterol, 635mg sodium.

Chicken Noodle Soup

A no-nonsense noodle soup. For variety, add other diced or frozen vegetables as desired.

PREP: 20 MINUTES PLUS COOLING   COOK: 25 MINUTES
MAKES ABOUT 9½ CUPS OR 4 MAIN-DISH SERVINGS

Basic Chicken Soup (opposite)   1 cup frozen peas
2 cups medium egg noodles (about   grated Parmesan or Pecorino Romano
   3 ounces)   cheese (optional)

1. Prepare Basic Chicken Soup as in Steps 1 and 2.
2. Meanwhile, prepare noodles in boiling water as label directs.
3. Complete soup as in Step 3, then heat through, adding cooked noodles and peas with shredded chicken. Serve with Parmesan cheese, if you like.

Each serving: About 290 calories, 26g protein, 33g carbohydrate, 6g total fat (1g saturated), 68mg cholesterol, 675mg sodium.

Asian Chicken Soup

An easy way to turn an old standard into a new dish

PREP: 25 MINUTES   COOK: 25 MINUTES

MAKES ABOUT 9 1/2 CUPS OR 4 MAIN-DISH SERVINGS

Basic Chicken Soup (page 76)
2 slices (1/8-inch-thick each) fresh ginger
1/2 cup regular long-grain rice
1 bunch watercress (about 6 ounces), tough stems trimmed

2 green onions, sliced
1 tablespoon soy sauce
1/2 teaspoon Asian sesame oil

1. Prepare Basic Chicken Soup, adding ginger with broth in Step 2.
2. Meanwhile, prepare rice as label directs.
3. With slotted spoon, remove ginger from soup and discard. Complete soup as in Step 3, adding cooked rice, watercress, green onions, soy sauce, and sesame oil to soup with shredded chicken.

Each serving: About 245 calories, 22g protein, 26g carbohydrate, 5g total fat (1g saturated), 4mg cholesterol, 900mg sodium.

Roman Egg-Drop Soup

With broth at the ready, this light-yet-satisfying soup couldn't be quicker. The cooked eggs look like little rags, or *straccetti* in Italian, lending this soup the name *stracciatelle* in its native city of Rome.

PREP: 5 MINUTES, NOT INCLUDING BROTH   COOK 5 MINUTES
MAKES ABOUT 5 1/2 CUPS OR 6 ACCOMPANIMENT SERVINGS

1 recipe Pressure-Cooker Chicken
Broth (page 75) or 3 cans (14 to
14 1/2 ounces each) chicken broth
(5 1/4 cups)
2 large eggs

1/4 cup freshly grated Parmesan or
Pecorino Romano cheese, plus
additional for serving
Ground black pepper
2 tablespoons finely chopped fresh
parsley

1. In a 3-quart saucepan, heat broth to boiling over high heat.
2. Meanwhile, in small bowl, with fork, beat eggs, 1/4 cup Parmesan, and 1/8 teaspoon pepper.
3. When chicken broth is boiling, reduce heat to low. Gradually add egg mixture to broth, stirring with fork just until egg sets and forms ribbons. Remove saucepan from heat; stir in parsley. Serve with additional grated Parmesan if you like.

Each serving: About 50 calories, 5g protein, 0g carbohydrate, 3g total fat (1g saturated), 0g fiber, 73mg cholesterol, 625mg sodium.

The Perfect Chicken-Noodle Soup

Treat your family to the real deal: chicken-noodle soup made from scratch. The kudos you'll get will be well worth the effort.

PREP: 45 MINUTES   COOK: ABOUT 2 HOURS 30 MINUTES

MAKES ABOUT 16 CUPS OR 8 MAIN-DISH SERVINGS

8 stalks celery

7 carrots, peeled

1 whole chicken (about 3 1/2 pounds)

2 pounds chicken leg quarters

1 medium onion, cut into pieces

1 garlic clove, cut in half

1/2 bunch parsley

8 sprigs thyme

20 whole black peppercorns

2 bay leaves

1 tablespoon salt

12 cups cold water

3 cups medium egg noodles, uncooked

1. Cut 4 stalks celery and 3 carrots crosswise into 2-inch pieces. In 8-quart saucepot, combine chicken, chicken neck, gizzards (not liver), chicken legs, celery and carrot pieces, onion, garlic, parsley, thyme, peppercorns, bay leaves, salt, and water; heat to boiling over high heat. Reduce heat to low and simmer, uncovered, 2 hours.

2. Meanwhile, cut remaining 4 stalks celery and 4 carrots crosswise into 1/4-inch-thick slices. Cook noodles as label directs; set aside.

3. Remove saucepot from heat; with tongs, transfer chicken to jelly-roll pan. Strain broth through colander into large bowl; discard solids. Skim fat and discard. Return broth to saucepot; heat to boiling over high heat.

4. Meanwhile, remove skin and bones from chicken and discard. Cut meat into 1/2-inch pieces.

5. When broth boils, add celery and carrot slices; heat to boiling. Reduce heat to medium-high; cook vegetables, uncovered, until very tender, about 10 minutes.

6. Remove from heat. Stir in cooked chicken and noodles.

Each serving: About 290 calories, 36g protein, 14g carbohydrate, 9g total fat (2g saturated), 115mg cholesterol, 945mg sodium.

The Perfect Chicken-Noodle Soup

Asian Chicken-Noodle Soup

Asian Chicken-Noodle Soup

This tastes just as good as, if not better than, any noodle-shop version. Use chopsticks or a fork to pick up the long noodles.

PREP: 15 MINUTES   COOK: 35 MINUTES

MAKES ABOUT 7 CUPS OR 4 MAIN-DISH SERVINGS

4 ounces rice noodles or linguine
3 cans (14 to 14 ounces each) chicken broth or 5 1/4 cups Chicken Broth (page 74)
3 small skinless, boneless chicken-breast halves (12 ounces)
4 ounces shiitake mushrooms, stems removed and caps thinly sliced
2 tablespoons soy sauce

1 tablespoon grated, peeled fresh ginger
3/4 teaspoon salt
1/8 teaspoon crushed red pepper
1/4 teaspoon Asian sesame oil
1 cup loosely packed fresh cilantro
2 green onions, trimmed and thinly sliced

1. Prepare noodles as label directs; drain.

2. Meanwhile, in 4-quart saucepan, heat broth to boiling over high heat. Add the chicken and reduce heat to low. Simmer until chicken is cooked through, about 15 minutes. Remove chicken with a slotted spoon and set aside to cool.

3. Stir mushrooms, soy sauce, ginger, salt, and crushed red pepper into broth. Simmer, uncovered, 10 minutes.

4. Cut chicken into thin strips. Add chicken, sesame oil, and cooked noodles to broth and heat through. Stir in cilantro and green onions.

Each serving: About 285 calories, 25g protein, 30g carbohydrate, 5g total fat (1g saturated), 58mg cholesterol, 1,050mg sodium.

Chicken Soup with Rice

Everyone loves this old favorite. A specialty of grandmas everywhere, it's like comfort in a bowl.

Prep: 10 minutes   Cook: 25 minutes

Makes about 8 cups or 4 main-dish servings

2/3 cup regular long-grain rice
3 cans (14 to 14 1/2 ounces each)
  chicken broth or 5 1/2 cups Chicken
  Broth (page 74)
3 carrots, peeled and cut into
  1/4-inch pieces

1 stalk celery, cut into 1/4-inch
  pieces
2 cups bite-size pieces cooked
  chicken (reserved from broth, if
  using homemade)
1 1/2 teaspoons salt

1. In 1-quart saucepan, prepare rice as label directs.

2. Meanwhile, in 3-quart saucepan, heat broth, carrots, and celery to boiling over high heat. Reduce heat to low; simmer, uncovered, until vegetables are tender, about 15 minutes. Stir in chicken, salt, and cooked rice; heat through.

Each serving: About 290 calories, 25g protein, 32g carbohydrate, 5g total fat (1g saturated), 58mg cholesterol, 960mg sodium.

Chicken Soup with Rice

After-Work Chicken Soup

You can whip up this homey chicken soup, made with leeks and bow-tie pasta, in just minutes!

PREP: 15 MINUTES   COOK: ABOUT 15 MINUTES

MAKES 8 CUPS OR 4 MAIN-DISH SERVINGS

1 leek (about 8 ounces)
1 tablespoon olive oil
2 carrots, peeled and each cut
   lengthwise in half, then crosswise
   into 1/4-inch-thick slices
1 stalk celery, thinly sliced
1/4 teaspoon dried thyme
1 bay leaf
1 can (14 to 14 1/2 ounces) chicken
   broth or 1 3/4 cups Chicken Broth
   (page 74)

1/2 cup small bow-tie pasta
   (2 ounces)
1/2 teaspoon salt
1/8 teaspoon ground black pepper
3 cups water
3 small skinless, boneless chicken
   breast halves (12 ounces), cut
   crosswise into very thin slices

1. Cut off root and trim dark green top from leek; cut leek lengthwise in half, then crosswise into 1/4-inch pieces. Rinse leek in large bowl of cold water, swishing to remove sand. Transfer to colander to drain, leaving sand in bottom of bowl.

2. In 4-quart saucepan, heat oil over medium-high heat until hot. Add leek, carrots, celery, thyme, and bay leaf; cook, stirring occasionally, until leek has wilted and vegetables are tender-crisp, 5 to 7 minutes.

3. Add broth, pasta, salt, pepper, and water; heat to boiling over high heat. Reduce heat to medium-low; simmer, covered, until pasta is just cooked, about 5 minutes. Increase heat to medium; add chicken and cook, uncovered, until chicken loses its pink color throughout, about 3 minutes. Discard bay leaf before serving.

Each serving: About 220 calories, 23g protein, 17g carbohydrate, 6g total fat (1g saturated), 63mg cholesterol, 800mg sodium.

Spring Ramen Noodle Soup

Quick, easy, and delicious—perfect for a novice cook or for anyone who has to get dinner on the table in a hurry.

PREP: 10 MINUTES   COOK: ABOUT 10 MINUTES

MAKES ABOUT 8 CUPS OR 4 MAIN-DISH SERVINGS

5 cups water
2 packages (3 ounces each) chicken-flavor or Oriental-flavor ramen noodle soup mix
6 ounces snow peas (about 2 cups)
2 green onions, trimmed

1 large carrot, peeled
4 small skinless, boneless chicken-breast halves (16 ounces)
1 teaspoon Asian sesame oil

1. In 4-quart saucepan, heat water and seasoning packets from ramen soup mix to boiling over high heat.

2. Meanwhile, remove strings from snow peas and cut each diagonally in half. Slice green onions and shred carrot. Cut chicken into 3/4-inch pieces. Break ramen noodle blocks into 2 layers.

3. Add snow peas, green onions, carrot, chicken, and noodles to boiling water mixture. Cook over high heat until chicken just loses its pink color throughout, 3 to 5 minutes. Remove saucepan from heat. Stir in sesame oil.

Each serving: About 355 calories, 32g protein, 32g carbohydrate, 11g total fat (4g saturated), 66mg cholesterol, 920mg sodium.

Mexican Chicken Soup

Mexican Chicken Soup

Add south-of-the-border flavor to a time-honored classic. For those who want a more authentic version, see page 100.

PREP: 25 MINUTES   COOK: 25 MINUTES
MAKES ABOUT 9 1/2 CUPS OR 4 MAIN-DISH SERVINGS

Basic Chicken Soup (page 76)
1/2 lime
1 cup fresh or frozen whole-kernel corn
1/2 cup loosely packed fresh cilantro, chopped

lime wedges, coarsely crushed tortilla chips, hot pepper sauce (optional)

1. Prepare Basic Chicken Soup, adding lime with broth in Step 2.
2. Complete soup as in Step 3, adding corn and cilantro with shredded chicken.
3. With slotted spoon, remove lime and squeeze juice into soup; discard lime. Serve soup with lime wedges, crushed tortilla chips, and hot pepper sauce, if you like.

Each serving: About 185 calories, 22g protein, 16g carbohydrate, 4g total fat (1g saturated), 41mg cholesterol, 640mg sodium.

Feel Full, Lose Weight

Looking to lose a few pounds? Indulge in soup. Research shows that the best way to start a meal may be with water- or broth-based soup. It fills you up—even more so than other foods low in calorie density. You'll feel full faster and end up eating less at that sitting. Or make soup a meal in itself; with vegetable-based soups, you'll get plenty of fiber to keep you feeling full longer.

Chicken and Escarole Soup with Meatballs

This soup is sometimes referred to as Italian Wedding Soup, but it really has nothing to do with weddings. The "wedding" refers to the "marriage" of its flavors.

PREP: 45 MINUTES   COOK: 1 HOUR 45 MINUTES

MAKES ABOUT 16 CUPS OR 14 FIRST-COURSE SERVINGS

1 chicken (4 pounds), cut into
 8 pieces
1 large onion (12 ounces), cut in half
1/4 teaspoon whole black
 peppercorns
1 bay leaf
12 cups water
1 pound ground meat for meat loaf
 (beef, pork, and veal)
2 garlic cloves, crushed with garlic
 press
1 large egg, beaten
1/4 cup chopped fresh parsley

1/2 teaspoon ground black pepper
3/4 cup grated Romano cheese, plus
 additional for serving
2 3/4 teaspoons salt
1 cup plain dried bread crumbs
1/3 cup milk
1 can (14 to 14 1/2 ounces) chicken
 broth or 1 3/4 cups Chicken Broth
 (page 74)
3 carrots, peeled and sliced
2 stalks celery, sliced
1 small head escarole (about 8
 ounces), cut into 1/2-inch strips

1. In 8-quart Dutch oven or saucepot, combine chicken, onion, peppercorns, bay leaf, and water; heat to boiling over high heat. Reduce heat to low; cover and simmer until chicken is tender, about 1 hour and 15 minutes.

2. Meanwhile, prepare meatballs: In large bowl, combine ground meat, garlic, egg, parsley, pepper, 1/2 cup Romano cheese, and 3/4 teaspoon salt just until well blended but not overmixed. In small bowl, with fork, mix bread crumbs and milk to form thick paste. Mix bread-crumb mixture into meat mixture just until blended. Shape mixture into 1-inch meatballs, handling meat as little as possible, and place 1 inch apart on cookie sheet; cover and refrigerate 30 minutes.

3. Transfer chicken to bowl; set aside until cool enough to handle.

Discard skin and bones from chicken; cut chicken into bite-size pieces. Reserve 2 cups cut-up chicken; refrigerate remaining chicken for another use. Strain broth through sieve into large bowl. Skim and discard fat from broth.

4. Return broth to same clean Dutch oven or saucepot. Add canned broth and 2 teaspoons salt; heat to boiling over high heat. Stir in carrots and celery; heat to boiling. Reduce heat to low; cover and simmer until vegetables are tender, 8 to 10 minutes. Add meatballs and 1/4 cup Romano cheese; heat to boiling over high heat. Reduce heat to low; cover and simmer until meatballs are cooked through, about 15 minutes. Stir in escarole and reserved chicken; heat through. Serve with grated Romano cheese.

Each serving: About 235 calories, 18g protein, 10g carbohydrate, 13g total fat (5g saturated), 61mg cholesterol, 760mg sodium.

Thai Chicken and Coconut Soup

This delectable soup is a winner when the weather is blustery.

PREP: 25 MINUTES   COOK: ABOUT 40 MINUTES

MAKES ABOUT 6 CUPS OR 4 MAIN-DISH SERVINGS

2 cans (14 to 14½ ounces each) chicken broth or 3½ cups Chicken Broth (page 74)
4 garlic cloves, crushed with garlic press
1 tablespoon Thai green curry paste
1 tablespoon minced, peeled fresh ginger
1 teaspoon coriander seeds
½ teaspoon whole black peppercorns
⅛ teaspoon cumin seeds
1 cup water

2 small skinless, boneless chicken-breast halves (8 ounces)
1 can (14 ounces) light unsweetened coconut milk (not cream of coconut), well stirred
1 cup thinly sliced shallots (about 5 large)
2 tablespoons Asian fish sauce (nuoc nam)
1 tablespoon fresh lime juice
2 tablespoons chopped fresh cilantro and/or dill
lime wedges (optional)

1. In 5-quart Dutch oven, heat broth, garlic, curry paste, ginger, coriander, peppercorns, cumin, and water to boiling over high heat. Reduce heat to low; cover and simmer 20 minutes. Strain broth through sieve into large bowl; discard solids. Set broth aside.

2. While broth is simmering, cut chicken breast into thin strips.

3. In same clean Dutch oven, heat ½ cup coconut milk to boiling over high heat; add shallots and cook, stirring occasionally, until shallots soften and liquid has evaporated. Reduce heat to medium; add chicken and cook, stirring constantly, until chicken just loses its pink color throughout.

4. Stir in strained broth, fish sauce, lime juice, and remaining coconut milk; heat through. Sprinkle soup with chopped cilantro. Serve with lime wedges, if you like.

Each serving: About 205 calories, 19g protein, 11g carbohydrate, 10g total fat (6g saturated), 33mg cholesterol, 1,325mg sodium.

Thai Chicken and Coconut Soup

Chicken Soup with Herbed Matzoh Balls

A Jewish classic with universal popularity.

PREP: 30 MINUTES PLUS CHILLING   COOK: 2 HOURS 15 MINUTES

MAKES 12 CUPS OR 10 FIRST-COURSE SERVINGS

CHICKEN BROTH
2 pounds chicken wings
2 stalks celery, cut crosswise into 2-inch pieces
3 carrots, peeled and cut crosswise into 2-inch pieces
1 small onion, cut lengthwise in half
1/4 teaspoon whole black peppercorns
1 bay leaf
3 cans (14 to 14 1/2 ounces each) chicken broth or 5 1/4 cups Chicken Broth (page 74)
4 cups water

MATZOH BALLS
1 cup unsalted matzoh meal
1/2 cup plain seltzer water
1 tablespoon vegetable oil
1 1/2 teaspoons salt
1/4 cup finely chopped fresh dill
1/4 cup finely chopped fresh parsley
1/4 cup eggs, lightly beaten

SOUP
1/4 cup minced fresh chives
1/4 cup chopped fresh dill
fresh dill and chives (optional)

1. Prepare Chicken Broth: In 6-quart Dutch oven or saucepot, combine chicken wings, celery, carrots, onion, peppercorns, bay leaf, broth, and water; heat to boiling over high heat. Reduce heat to low and simmer, partially covered, 45 minutes, skimming foam occasionally.

2. Meanwhile, prepare Matzoh Balls: In large bowl, with fork, stir matzoh meal, seltzer, oil, salt, dill, parsley, and egg just until evenly mixed. Cover bowl with plastic wrap and refrigerate 30 minutes.

3. Strain Chicken Broth through sieve into large bowl, pressing on solids with back of spoon to extract as much liquid as possible; discard solids. Cover and refrigerate Broth overnight or until cold enough to remove fat from surface. Refrigerate up to 3 days or freeze up to 3 weeks. Makes about 9 cups Broth.

4. In 8-quart saucepot, heat *2 quarts water* to boiling over high heat.

5. Meanwhile, with damp hands, shape matzoh-meal mixture into forty-eight 1-inch balls and place 1 inch apart in 15 1/2" by 10 1/2" jelly-roll pan. (Matzoh-ball mixture is very wet; you will need to moisten hands often while shaping mixture into balls.)

6. Reduce heat under saucepot to bring water to a gentle boil. With damp hands, drop matzoh balls, one by one, into water in saucepot; reheat just to boiling. Reduce heat to low; cover and simmer until matzoh balls are tender and cooked through, 45 to 55 minutes.

7. With strainer or slotted spoon, transfer matzoh balls to paper towels to drain, then transfer to clean jelly-roll pan. Use immediately or cover and refrigerate up to 2 days. Or place matzoh balls 1 inch apart on jelly-roll pan; cover and freeze until firm. Once frozen, transfer balls to freezer-weight ziptight bag or plastic container and freeze up to 3 weeks.

8. To serve, remove and discard any fat from chilled broth. In 4-quart saucepan, heat broth to boiling over high heat. Add matzoh balls; heat to boiling. Reduce heat to low; cover and simmer until matzoh balls are heated through, about 5 minutes (10 minutes if frozen). Stir in chives and dill. Garnish with more herbs, if you like.

Each serving: About 105 calories, 7g protein, 10g carbohydrate, 3g total fat (1g saturated), 71mg cholesterol, 695mg sodium.

Greek Lemon Soup

Called *avgolemono* in Greek, this velvety-smooth chicken soup is thickened with eggs and rice. It's best served soon after you make it.

PREP: 10 MINUTES   COOK: 40 MINUTES

MAKES ABOUT 6 CUPS OR 6 FIRST-COURSE SERVINGS

2 cans (14 to 14 1/2 ounces each) chicken broth or 3 1/2 cups Chicken Broth (page 74)

1 skinless, boneless chicken-breast half (about 6 ounces)

1 small onion, peeled and studded with 2 whole cloves

1 carrot, trimmed, peeled, and cut into 2-inch pieces

1 stalk celery, trimmed and cut into 2-inch pieces

2 1/2 cups water

2/3 cup regular long-grain rice

3 large eggs

1/3 cup fresh lemon juice (about 2 large lemons)

1 tablespoon butter or margarine

chopped fresh chives (optional)

1. In 3-quart saucepan, heat broth, chicken, onion, carrot, celery, and water to boiling over high heat. Reduce heat to low; cover and simmer 10 minutes.

2. With slotted spoon, remove chicken and vegetables from saucepan; discard vegetables. Cool chicken until easy to handle. Shred into thin strips then set aside.

3. Add rice to simmering broth; heat to boiling over high heat. Reduce heat to low; cover and simmer until rice is tender, 15 to 20 minutes.

4. Meanwhile, in large bowl, with wire whisk, mix eggs and lemon juice until combined.

5. Whisk 2 cups simmering broth slowly into bowl with egg mixture, whisking constantly. Return broth and egg mixture to saucepan; heat just to simmering, whisking constantly (do not boil or soup will curdle), about 5 minutes.

6. Stir in shredded chicken and butter or margarine. Sprinkle with chopped chives to serve, if you like.

Each serving: About 185 calories, 14g protein, 18g carbohydrate, 6g total fat (3g saturated), 129mg cholesterol, 504mg sodium.

Chicken and
Red Potato Chowder

This creamy chowder calls for rotisserie chicken meat instead of seafood, which cuts down on preparation time but not on flavor.

PREP: 20 MINUTES   COOK: ABOUT 35 MINUTES

MAKES ABOUT 8 1/2 CUPS OR 4 MAIN-DISH SERVINGS

3 slices bacon, cut crosswise into 1/2-inch pieces
1 medium onion, chopped
2 stalks celery, cut into 1/4-inch pieces
1 pound baby red potatoes, cut into 1/4-inch-thick slices
2 cans (14 to 14 1/2 ounces each) chicken broth or 3 1/2 cups Chicken Broth (page 74)

1/4 teaspoon dried thyme
1/8 teaspoon ground black pepper
2 cups (3/4-inch pieces) cooked skinless rotisserie chicken meat (10 ounces)
1 cup frozen whole-kernel corn
1 small tomato, cut into 1/2-inch pieces
1 cup half-and-half or light cream

1. In 5- to 6-quart saucepot, cook bacon over medium heat until browned. With slotted spoon, transfer bacon to paper towels to drain.

2. To drippings in saucepot, add onion and celery and cook, stirring occasionally, until vegetables are lightly browned, 5 to 8 minutes.

3. Add potatoes, broth, thyme, and pepper; heat to boiling over high heat. Reduce heat to low; cover and simmer until potatoes are tender, 10 to 12 minutes.

4. Gently stir in chicken, frozen corn, and tomato; heat to boiling over high heat. Reduce heat to low; cover and simmer 5 minutes. Stir in half-and-half; heat through.

5. To serve, sprinkle with bacon.

Each serving: About 550 calories, 31g protein, 39g carbohydrate, 31g total fat (12g saturated), 104mg cholesterol, 195mg sodium.

South-of-the-Border Chicken Soup

A heartier, more flavorful alternative to Mexican Chicken Soup (page 91), this thicker version is full of mashed and diced potatoes, seasoned with fresh lime juice, and topped with avocado. Except for the finishing touches (in Step 5), this can be made a day ahead.

PREP: 1 HOUR   COOK: 25 MINUTES

MAKES ABOUT 16 CUPS OR 8 MAIN-DISH SERVINGS

8 medium all-purpose potatoes (2¹/₂ pounds)
1 chicken (4 pounds), cut into 8 pieces
3 large stalks celery, each trimmed and cut into thirds
3 carrots (¹/₂ pound), each peeled, trimmed, and cut into thirds
2 medium onions, unpeeled and each cut into quarters
10 cups water
10 sprigs cilantro plus ¹/₄ cup chopped fresh cilantro
2 bay leaves

1 teaspoon whole black peppercorns
1 can (15¹/₄ to 16 ounces) whole-kernel corn, drained
2 teaspoons salt
¹/₄ cup fresh lime juice (about 2 large limes)
garnishes: 2 ripe medium avocados, cut into ¹/₂-inch cubes; tortilla chips; lime wedges; cilantro sprigs

1. Peel 3 potatoes. In 8-quart Dutch oven or saucepot, combine chicken, celery, carrots, onions, cilantro sprigs, bay leaves, peppercorns, peeled potatoes, and water; heat to boiling over high heat. Reduce heat to low; cover and simmer until chicken loses its pink color throughout and vegetables are tender, 35 to 45 minutes.

2. With slotted spoon, transfer chicken and potatoes to separate bowls. Strain broth through sieve into large bowl; discard vegetables. Skim and discard fat from broth; return broth to same clean Dutch oven. Mash cooked potatoes with 1 cup broth; stir mashed-potato mixture into broth in Dutch oven.

3. Peel and chop remaining 5 potatoes. Add potatoes to broth; heat to boiling over high heat. Reduce heat to low; cover and simmer until potatoes are fork-tender, about 10 minutes.

4. Meanwhile, discard skin and bones from chicken; cut chicken into bite-size pieces. Stir chicken, corn, and salt into broth; heat through.
5. Just before serving, stir lime juice and chopped cilantro into soup. Serve soup with garnishes.

Each serving without garnishes: About 325 calories, 29g protein, 28g carbohydrate, 11g total fat (3g saturated), 71mg cholesterol, 735mg sodium.

South-of-the-Border Chicken Soup

Coq au Vin

This well-known dish, basically chicken stewed in a red-wine sauce, is a specialty of the Burgundy region of France. If possible, use a moderately priced California or Oregon Pinot Noir, which is made from the same grape as the more expensive French Burgundy.

PREP: 45 MINUTES   COOK/BAKE: ABOUT 1 HOUR 30 MINUTES
MAKES 6 MAIN-DISH SERVINGS

4 slices bacon, cut into 1/2-inch pieces
4 pounds chicken parts (thighs, drumsticks, and/or breasts), skin removed
1/2 teaspoon salt
1/4 teaspoon coarsely ground pepper
1 small onion, finely chopped
1 carrot, peeled and finely chopped
1 stalk celery, finely chopped
20 pearl onions (about half 10-ounce package or generous 1 cup), soaked in warm water and peeled

1 package (12 ounces) mushrooms, trimmed and each cut in half or into quarters if large
2 tablespoons butter or margarine
3 tablespoons all-purpose flour
1 1/2 cups dry red wine
1/2 can (8 ounces) chicken broth or 1 cup Chicken Broth (page 74)
2 tablespoons tomato paste
2 bay leaves
1/2 cup loosely packed fresh parsley, chopped

1. Preheat oven to 325°F. In 5-quart Dutch oven, cook bacon over medium heat until browned. With slotted spoon, transfer bacon to paper towels to drain.

2. Sprinkle chicken with salt and pepper. To drippings in Dutch oven, add half of chicken and cook over medium-high heat until well browned on all sides, about 10 minutes, using slotted spoon to transfer chicken to large bowl as it is browned. Repeat with remaining chicken.

3. To same Dutch oven, add chopped onion, carrot, and celery and cook, stirring occasionally, until vegetables are tender, about 10 minutes. With slotted spoon, transfer to bowl with chicken. Add pearl onions and mushrooms to Dutch oven and cook, stirring occasionally, until browned, about 8 minutes. Transfer to bowl with chicken.

4. In same Dutch oven, melt butter. Add flour and cook, stirring frequently, 2 minutes. With wire whisk, whisk in wine until smooth. Stir in broth and tomato paste. Heat to boiling, whisking frequently; boil 2 minutes.

5. Return chicken, vegetables, and three-fourths of bacon to Dutch oven. Add bay leaves; heat to boiling. Cover Dutch oven and bake, turning chicken once during baking, until chicken is very tender and juices run clear when thickest part of thigh is pierced with tip of knife, 40 to 45 minutes.

6. To serve, discard bay leaves. Skim and discard fat. Transfer stew to large serving bowl; sprinkle with parsley and remaining bacon.

Each serving: About 330 calories, 36g protein, 13g carbohydrate, 14g total fat (6g saturated), 108mg cholesterol, 573mg sodium.

Coq au Vin

Quick Cassoulet

We cut the prep time of this slow-baked French casserole by using store-bought cooked chicken and canned beans. The stew simmers briefly on the stovetop to meld flavors.

PREP: 15 MINUTES   COOK: ABOUT 20 MINUTES

MAKES ABOUT 10 CUPS, OR 6 MAIN-DISH SERVINGS

1 tablespoon olive oil
8 ounces Italian-style turkey-sausage links, each cut into 1-inch pieces
8 ounces peeled baby carrots (half 16-ounce bag), each cut into thirds
2 stalks celery, chopped
1 medium onion, chopped
1/4 teaspoon dried thyme
3 cans (15 to 19 ounces each) white kidney beans (cannellini), rinsed and drained

1 can (14 to 14 1/2 ounces) chicken broth or 1 3/4 cups Chicken Broth (page 74)
2 packages (about 4 ounces each) roasted chicken-breast halves, skin and bones discarded, meat torn into 1-inch pieces
1/2 cup water

1. In nonstick 5- to 6-quart Dutch oven, heat oil over medium-high heat until hot. Add sausage, carrots, celery, onion, and thyme, and cook until lightly browned, 12 to 15 minutes.

2. Add beans, broth, chicken, and water to Dutch oven; heat to boiling over high heat, stirring gently to combine. Reduce heat to low; cover and simmer 5 minutes.

Each serving: About 365 calories, 26g protein, 44g carbohydrate, 9g total fat (2g saturated), 42mg cholesterol, 965mg sodium.

Southwest Chicken Stew

A flavor-packed combo of chicken thighs, potatoes, corn, and beans is simmered together, then thickened with crushed tortilla chips.

PREP: 25 MINUTES   COOK: ABOUT 30 MINUTES
MAKES 6 MAIN-DISH SERVINGS

1 teaspoon olive oil
6 large bone-in chicken thighs (about 2 pounds), skin and excess fat removed
1 medium onion, chopped
2 jalapeño chiles, seeded and minced
2 garlic cloves, crushed with garlic press
3/4 teaspoon ground cumin
1/2 teaspoon dried oregano
1 pound medium red potatoes, cut into 1 1/2-inch pieces

1 can (15 to 19 ounces) white kidney beans (cannellini), rinsed and drained
1 can (15 1/4 ounces) whole-kernel corn, drained
1 can (14 to 14 1/2 ounces) chicken broth or 1 3/4 cups Chicken Broth (page 74)
1 teaspoon salt
1/4 cup crushed baked tortilla chips
1/2 cup loosely packed fresh cilantro, chopped

1. In deep, nonstick 12-inch skillet, heat oil over medium-high heat until hot. Add chicken and cook until browned on both sides, 6 to 8 minutes, using slotted spoon to transfer chicken to plate as it is browned.

2. To same skillet, add onion, jalapeños, garlic, cumin, and oregano and cook over medium heat, covered, until onion is golden, stirring occasionally, about 5 minutes.

3. Return chicken to skillet. Add potatoes, beans, corn, broth, and salt; heat to boiling. Reduce heat to medium-low and simmer, covered, until potatoes are fork-tender and juices run clear when thickest part of chicken thigh is pierced with tip of knife, stirring occasionally, about 15 minutes.

4. Stir in tortilla chips and cook, uncovered, about until mixture thickens slightly, 2 minutes. Add cilantro just before serving.

Each serving: About 365 calories, 31g protein, 44g carbohydrate, 7g total fat (2g saturated), 98mg cholesterol, 1,115mg sodium.

Chicken and Vegetable Stew with Chive Dumplings

This dish is full of old-fashioned midwestern goodness. Most traditional versions of this recipe call for a mature stewing hen or fowl—a tough, old but flavorful bird that takes several hours to cook; we've substituted quick-cooking chicken breasts.

PREP: 30 MINUTES   COOK: 1 HOUR   MAKES 6 MAIN-DISH SERVINGS

STEW
2 teaspoons sweet paprika
$1/2$ teaspoon salt
6 bone-in chicken-breast halves
   (about $3 1/2$ pounds), skin removed
2 tablespoons olive oil
3 medium leeks (about 1 pound)
3 large carrots, peeled and cut into
   $1/4$-inch pieces
2 large stalks celery, cut into
   $1/4$-inch pieces
1 tablespoon all purpose-flour
1 cup water

2 cans (14 to $14 1/2$ ounces each)
   chicken broth or $3 1/2$ cups Chicken
   Broth (page 74)
$3/4$ cup milk
1 package (10 ounces) frozen peas

CHIVE DUMPLINGS
2 cups all-purpose flour
$1/2$ cup minced fresh chives
2 teaspoons baking powder
$1/2$ teaspoon salt
$1/4$ cup vegetable shortening
1 cup milk

1. Prepare Stew: In cup, with fork, mix paprika and salt; sprinkle evenly over chicken breasts.

2. In 8-quart Dutch oven, heat 1 tablespoon oil over medium-high heat until hot. Add half of chicken, and cook until lightly browned on all sides, about 8 minutes, using slotted spoon to transfer chicken to bowl as it is browned. Repeat with remaining chicken; reserve drippings.

3. Meanwhile, cut off roots and trim dark green tops from leeks; cut each leek lengthwise in half, then crosswise into 1/4-inch pieces. Rinse in large bowl of cold water, swishing to remove any sand. Transfer to colander to drain, leaving sand in bottom of bowl.

4. Add remaining 1 tablespoon oil to drippings in Dutch oven and heat over medium heat until hot. Add carrots and celery, and cook, stirring occasionally, until vegetables are lightly browned, about 10 minutes.

Chicken and Vegetable Stew with Chive Dumplings

Add leeks and cook, stirring occasionally, until vegetables are tender and leeks are golden, about 10 minutes longer.

5. In cup, with wire whisk or fork, stir flour and water until blended. Add flour mixture and broth to Dutch oven; heat to boiling over high heat, stirring occasionally. Return chicken to Dutch oven and heat to boiling.

6. Meanwhile, prepare Dumplings: In medium bowl, with wire whisk, mix flour, chives, baking powder, and salt. With pastry blender or two knives used scissor-fashion, cut in shortening until well mixed. Stir in milk just until blended.

7. Drop dumpling mixture by scant 1/4 cups into boiling stew to make 12 dumplings. Cover; reduce heat to low and simmer until juices run clear when thickest part of chicken breast is pierced with tip of knife and dumplings are cooked through and tender, about 25 minutes.
8. To complete stew, stir in milk and peas; heat through.

Each serving: About 605 calories, 50g protein, 56g carbohydrate, 20g total fat (5g saturated), 106mg cholesterol, 1,315mg sodium.

Stewing Secret

What's the difference between a thick, delicious stew and one that's just not very gutsy? Browning. Meat for stew needs to be seared to get that gorgeous color and to caramelize the proteins and sugars. To brown it perfectly, dry the meat well with paper towels, heat oil until it's very hot, and add the chunks in small batches. This way, moisture can evaporate and the pieces will sear, not steam.

Chicken and Sweet Potato Stew

Coat chicken thighs with a fragrant mix of cumin and cinnamon, then simmer with beta carotene–rich sweet potatoes in a creamy peanut-butter sauce—delectable over brown rice.

PREP: 20 MINUTES   COOK: 45 MINUTES   MAKES 4 MAIN-DISH SERVINGS

4 bone-in chicken thighs (about 1¹/₂ pounds), skin removed
1 teaspoon ground cumin
¹/₄ teaspoon ground cinnamon
1 tablespoon olive oil
3 medium sweet potatoes (about 1¹/₂ pounds), peeled and cut into ¹/₂-inch pieces
1 medium onion, sliced

1 can (28 ounces) whole tomatoes in juice
3 tablespoons natural peanut butter
¹/₂ teaspoon salt
¹/₄ teaspoon crushed red pepper
2 garlic cloves, peeled
¹/₄ cup packed fresh cilantro leaves plus 2 tablespoons chopped

1. Rub chicken thighs with cumin and cinnamon; set aside.

2. In nonstick 12-inch skillet, heat oil over medium heat until hot. Add sweet potatoes and onion and cook, stirring occasionally, until onion is tender, 12 to 15 minutes. Transfer sweet-potato mixture to plate.

3. Increase heat to medium-high. Add seasoned chicken, and cook until chicken is lightly browned on both sides, about 5 minutes.

4. Meanwhile, drain tomatoes, reserving juice. Coarsely chop tomatoes and set aside. In blender or in food processor with knife blade attached, puree tomato juice, peanut butter, salt, crushed red pepper, garlic, and ¹/₄ cup cilantro leaves until smooth.

5. Add sweet-potato mixture, peanut-butter sauce, and chopped tomatoes to skillet with chicken; heat to boiling over high heat. Reduce heat to low; cover and simmer until juices run clear when thickest part of chicken thigh is pierced with tip of knife, about 25 minutes.

6. To serve, sprinkle with chopped cilantro.

Each serving: About 410 calories, 26g protein, 50g carbohydrate, 12g total fat (2g saturated), 76mg cholesterol, 725mg sodium.

Moroccan-Style Chicken Stew

Moroccan-Style Chicken Stew

This traditionally long-simmering stew, called a tagine, is rich with a blend of spices, olives, and raisins. Our version cooks quickly thanks to small chunks of tender chicken and canned beans.

PREP: 15 MINUTES   COOK: 20 MINUTES
MAKES ABOUT 8 CUPS OR 6 MAIN-DISH SERVINGS

1 tablespoon olive oil
1 medium onion, chopped
1 tablespoon all-purpose flour
1 teaspoon ground coriander
1 teaspoon ground cumin
1/2 teaspoon salt
1/4 teaspoon ground red pepper
  (cayenne)
1/4 teaspoon ground cinnamon
1 1/2 pounds skinless, boneless
  chicken thighs, cut into 2-inch
  pieces

2 garlic cloves, crushed with garlic
  press
1 can (28 ounces) whole tomatoes
  in puree
1 can (15 to 19 ounces) garbanzo
  beans, rinsed and drained
1/3 cup dark seedless raisins
1/4 cup salad olives (chopped
  pimiento-stuffed olives)
1 cup water
1/2 cup loosely packed fresh cilantro

1. In nonstick 5- to 6-quart Dutch oven, heat oil over medium heat until hot. Add onion and cook until light golden, about 5 minutes.
2. Meanwhile, in pie plate, mix flour, coriander, cumin, salt, pepper, and cinnamon. Add chicken and toss with flour mixture until evenly coated.
3. Add chicken to Dutch oven and cook until lightly browned, about 4 minutes per side. Add garlic and cook 1 minute.
4. Stir in tomatoes with their puree, beans, raisins, olives, and water. Simmer, uncovered, until juices run clear when thickest part of chicken is pierced with tip of knife, about 5 minutes, breaking up tomatoes with side of spoon. Garnish with cilantro.

Each serving: About 305 calories, 29g protein, 28g carbohydrate, 9g total fat (2g saturated), 94mg cholesterol, 890mg sodium.

Hearty Chicken and Vegetable Stew

All you need to round out the meal is a mixed green salad.

PREP: 45 MINUTES   COOK: 1 HOUR   MAKES 4 MAIN-DISH SERVINGS

2 medium leeks
2 tablespoons olive oil
2 tablespoons butter or margarine
4 small skinless, boneless chicken
   breast halves (16 ounces), cut into
   1 1/2-inch pieces
8 ounces mushrooms, trimmed and
   thickly sliced
3 carrots (about 8 ounces), trimmed,
   peeled, and cut into 1-inch pieces
1 fennel bulb (about 1 pound),
   trimmed and cut lengthwise into
   thin wedges

3/4 pound red potatoes, cut into
   1-inch pieces
1 bay leaf
1/4 teaspoon dried tarragon
1/2 cup dry white wine
1 can (14 to 14 1/2 ounces) chicken
   broth or 1 3/4 cups Chicken Broth
   (page 74)
1/4 cup water
3/4 cup half-and-half or light cream
3 tablespoons all-purpose flour
1 cup frozen peas, thawed
3/4 teaspoon salt

1. Cut off roots and trim dark green tops from leeks; cut each leek lengthwise in half, then cut crosswise into 3/4-inch pieces. Rinse leeks in large bowl of cold water, swishing to remove any sand. Transfer to colander to drain, leaving sand in bottom of bowl.

2. In 5-quart Dutch oven or saucepot, heat 1 tablespoon oil and 1 tablespoon butter over medium-high heat until butter has melted and oil is hot. Add chicken and cook until chicken is golden and just loses its pink color throughout, about 12 to 15 minutes, using slotted spoon to transfer chicken to medium bowl as it is browned.

3. To drippings in Dutch oven, add mushrooms and cook until golden (do not overbrown), about 10 minutes. Transfer mushrooms to bowl with chicken.

4. To Dutch oven, add remaining 1 tablespoon oil and remaining 1 tablespoon butter; heat until hot. Add carrots, leeks, fennel, potatoes, bay leaf, and tarragon; cook, stirring occasionally, until fennel is translucent and leeks have wilted, 10 to 15 minutes.

5. Add wine; cook, stirring, 2 minutes. Add broth and water; heat to boiling over high heat. Reduce heat to low; cover and simmer until vegetables are tender, about 20 minutes.

6. In cup, with fork, mix half-and-half and flour until smooth. Stir half-and-half mixture into vegetable mixture; heat to boiling over high heat. Reduce heat to medium; cook until slightly thickened, about 1 minute. Stir in chicken, mushrooms, peas, and salt; heat through. Discard bay leaf.

Each serving: About 530 calories, 37g protein, 53g carbohydrate, 20g total fat (5g saturated), 85mg cholesterol, 985mg sodium.

The Skinny on Poultry

The breast is the most tender part of the bird—and also the leanest. A 3 1/2-ounce portion of breast meat without the skin has about 4 grams of fat. The same amount of skinless dark meat has about 10 grams of fat. And keep in mind that removing poultry skin slashes the amount of fat almost in half.

Chicken Bouillabaisse

An easy, affordable version of the classic French fish stew; we used skinned chicken thighs instead of the traditional assortment of fish.

PREP: 1 HOUR   COOK: 30 MINUTES   MAKES 4 MAIN-DISH SERVINGS

1 tablespoon olive oil
8 medium bone-in chicken thighs (about 2$^{1}/_{2}$ pounds), skin and excess fat removed
2 large carrots, peeled and finely chopped
1 medium onion, finely chopped
1 medium fennel bulb (1$^{1}/_{4}$ pounds), trimmed and cut crosswise into $^{1}/_{4}$-inch-thick slices
$^{1}/_{2}$ cup water
3 garlic cloves, minced
1 can (14 to 14$^{1}/_{2}$ ounces) diced tomatoes

1 can (14 to 14$^{1}/_{2}$ ounces) chicken broth or 1$^{3}/_{4}$ cups Chicken Broth (page 74)
$^{1}/_{2}$ cup dry white wine
2 tablespoons anisette (anise-flavored liqueur; optional)
$^{1}/_{2}$ teaspoon salt
$^{1}/_{4}$ teaspoon dried thyme
$^{1}/_{8}$ teaspoon ground red pepper (cayenne)
1 bay leaf
pinch saffron threads

1. In 5-quart Dutch oven, heat oil over medium-high heat until hot. Add chicken in batches, and cook until well browned, about 5 minutes per batch, using slotted spoon to transfer chicken thighs to large bowl as they are browned.

2. Add carrots and onion to Dutch oven and cook over medium heat, stirring occasionally, until tender and golden, about 10 minutes. Transfer to bowl with chicken.

3. Preheat oven to 350°F. Add fennel and water to Dutch oven, stirring until browned bits are loosened from bottom of pan. Cook, stirring occasionally, until fennel is tender and browned, about 7 minutes. Add garlic and cook 3 minutes longer.

4. Return chicken and carrot mixture to Dutch oven. Add tomatoes with their juice, broth, white wine, anisette, if using, salt, thyme, ground red pepper, bay leaf, and saffron; heat to boiling over high heat. Cover and bake until juices run clear when thickest part of chicken thigh is pierced with tip of knife, about 30 minutes. Discard bay leaf.

Each serving: About 310 calories, 32g protein, 24g carbohydrate, 10g total fat (2g saturated), 119mg cholesterol, 935mg sodium.

Chicken Bouillabaisse

BEEF, PORK & LAMB

Beef and Wild Mushroom
Stew, page 130

Brown Beef Stock

For a richer, meatier flavor, use four pounds of beef bones and one pound of oxtails.

PREP: 5 MINUTES   COOK: 7 HOURS 30 MINUTES   MAKES ABOUT 5 CUPS

5 pounds beef bones, cut into 3-inch
  pieces
2 medium onions, each cut in half
3 carrots, peeled and cut in half
2 stalks celery, cut in half

13 cups water
1 small bunch parsley
1 bay leaf
1/2 teaspoon dried thyme

1. Preheat oven to 450°F. Spread beef bones, onions, carrots, and celery in large roasting pan (17 1/2" by 11 1/2"). Roast, stirring every 15 minutes, until well browned, about 1 hour.

2. With tongs, transfer browned bones and vegetables to 6-quart saucepot. Carefully pour off fat from roasting pan. Add 1 cup water to roasting pan and heat to boiling, stirring until browned bits are loosened from bottom of pan; add to pot. Add remaining 12 cups water, parsley, bay leaf, and thyme to pot. Heat to boiling over high heat, skimming foam from surface. Reduce heat and simmer, skimming foam occasionally, 6 hours.

3. Strain broth through colander into large bowl; discard solids. Strain again through fine-mesh sieve into containers. Cool. Cover and refrigerate to use within 3 days, or freeze up to 4 months.

4. To use, skim and discard fat from surface of stock.

Each cup: About 39 calories, 5g protein, 5g carbohydrate, 0g total fat (0g saturated), 0mg cholesterol, 73mg sodium.

Beef and Barley Soup

One batch serves a party of eight. But we like to cook this hearty soup over the weekend and freeze it in family-size portions for quick weeknight dinners.

PREP: 45 MINUTES   COOK: 2 HOURS 30 MINUTES
MAKES ABOUT 16 CUPS OR 8 MAIN-DISH SERVINGS

1 tablespoon plus 4 teaspoons vegetable oil
3 medium celery stalks, finely chopped
1 large onion (12 ounces), finely chopped
1 1/2 pounds boneless beef chuck, cut into 1/2-inch pieces
1/2 teaspoon salt
2 cans (14 to 14 1/2 ounces each) beef broth or 3 1/2 cups Brown Beef Stock (opposite)
1 can (14 to 14 1/2 ounces) diced tomatoes

6 cups water
1 cup pearl barley
5 medium carrots (12 ounces), peeled and cut crosswise into 1/4-inch-thick slices
5 medium parsnips (12 ounces), peeled and cut crosswise into 1/4-inch-thick slices
2 medium turnips (8 ounces), peeled and finely chopped
3 strips (3" by 1" each) orange peel
pinch ground cloves

1. In 8-quart Dutch oven, heat 1 tablespoon vegetable oil over high heat until hot. Add celery and onion and cook, stirring occasionally, until tender and golden, about 10 minutes; transfer vegetables to bowl.

2. Pat beef dry with paper towels. In same Dutch oven, heat 2 teaspoons oil over high heat until hot. Add half of beef and cook until well browned using slotted spoon to transfer beef to plate as it is browned. Repeat with remaining 2 teaspoons oil and beef.

3. Return beef to Dutch oven. Stir in salt, celery mixture, broth, tomatoes with their juice, and water; heat to boiling over high heat. Reduce heat to low; cover and simmer 1 hour.

4. Add barley, carrots, parsnips, turnips, orange peel, and cloves; heat to boiling over high heat. Reduce heat to low; cover and simmer until beef, barley, and vegetables are tender, 50 to 60 minutes.

Each serving: About 320 calories, 25g protein, 36g carbohydrate, 9g total fat (3g saturated), 41mg cholesterol, 740mg sodium.

Country Beef and Veggie Soup

This is so filling it can almost be considered a stew. Serve with crusty farmhouse white bread for a cozy Sunday supper.

PREP: 25 MINUTES PLUS SOAKING BEANS   COOK: 1 HOUR 45 MINUTES

MAKES ABOUT 14 CUPS OR 8 MAIN-DISH SERVINGS

8 ounces dry large lima beans (1 1/2 cups), rinsed and picked through
1 tablespoon vegetable oil
2 pounds beef shank cross cuts, each 1 1/2 inches thick
2 medium onions, finely chopped
3 garlic cloves, minced
1/8 teaspoon ground cloves
4 large carrots, peeled and cut into 1/2-inch pieces
2 large stalks celery, cut into 1/2-inch pieces
8 ounces green cabbage (about 1/2 small head), cored and cut into 1/2-inch pieces (about 5 cups)

1 can (14 to 14 1/2 ounces) beef broth, or 1 3/4 cups Brown Beef Stock (page 116)
2 teaspoons salt
1/2 teaspoon dried thyme leaves
1/2 teaspoon ground black pepper
4 1/2 cups water
3 medium all-purpose potatoes (1 pound), peeled and cut into 3/4-inch pieces
1 can (14 to 14 1/2 ounces) diced tomatoes
1 cup frozen whole-kernel corn
1 cup frozen peas
1/4 cup chopped fresh parsley

1. In large bowl, place beans and enough *water* to cover by 2 inches. Soak overnight. (Or, in 4-quart saucepan, heat beans and enough *water* to cover by 2 inches to boiling over high heat; cook 2 minutes. Remove from heat; cover and let stand 1 hour.) Drain and rinse beans.

2. In 8-quart Dutch oven, heat vegetable oil over medium-high heat until hot. Add half of beef shanks and cook until meat is well browned, using slotted spoon to transfer beef shanks to plate as it is browned. Repeat with remaining beef.

3. Reduce heat to medium; add onions and cook, stirring occasionally, until tender, about 5 minutes. Add garlic and cloves; cook, stirring, 30 seconds. Return beef to Dutch oven. Stir in carrots, celery, cabbage, broth, salt, thyme, pepper, and water; heat to boiling over high heat. Reduce heat to low; cover and simmer until beef is tender, about 1 hour.

(continued on page 120)

Country Beef and Veggie Soup

4. Meanwhile, in 4-quart saucepan, heat beans and *5 cups water* to boiling over high heat. Reduce heat to low; cover and simmer until beans are tender, about 30 minutes. Drain beans.

5. Add potatoes and cooked beans to cooked beef; heat to boiling over high heat. Reduce heat to low; cover and simmer 5 minutes. Stir in tomatoes with their juice; cover and simmer until potatoes are tender, about 10 minutes longer.

6. With slotted spoon, transfer beef shanks to plate; set aside until cool enough to handle. Remove and discard bones and fat; cut beef into 1/2-inch pieces. Return beef to Dutch oven. Add frozen corn and peas; heat through. To serve, sprinkle with parsley.

Each serving: About 375 calories, 27g protein, 44g carbohydrate, 11g total fat (4g saturated), 38mg cholesterol, 990mg sodium.

Fixing a Salty Soup or Stew

Try this quick trick if you've over-salted a pot of soup or stew: Peel and quarter a potato and simmer in the soup or stew for 10 to 15 minutes; remove before serving. The potato's starchy texture should absorb the excess salt—unless you *really* dumped in a lot, in which case you may be stuck with a salty dish.

Sausage, Squash, and Bean Soup

PREP: 25 MINUTES   COOK: ABOUT 1 1/2 HOURS
MAKES ABOUT 14 CUPS OR 8 MAIN-DISH SERVINGS

1 pound sweet Italian-sausage links, casing removed

1 large onion, chopped

3 medium carrots, cut into 1/4-inch-thick slices

2 large stalks celery, cut into 1/4-inch pieces

3 large garlic cloves, crushed with press

2 cans (15 to 19 ounces each) white kidney beans (cannellini), rinsed and drained

1 can (14 to 14 1/2 ounces) chicken broth, or 1 3/4 cups Chicken Broth (page 74)

4 cups water

Ground black pepper

1 medium butternut squash (1 1/2-2 pounds), peeled, seeded, and cut into 1-inch-chunks

1 small head escarole (10 ounces) cut into 1 1/2-inch pieces

1. In 6- to 8-quart Dutch oven, cook sausage over medium-high heat 6 to 8 minutes or until browned, stirring to break up sausage with side of spoon. Pour off fat. Stir in onion; cook 10 minutes or until onion is browned, stirring frequently.

2. Stir in carrots, celery, and garlic; cook 1 minute. Stir in beans, broth, water, and 1/8 teaspoon pepper; heat to boiling over high heat. Reduce heat to low; cover and simmer 30 minutes, stirring occasionally.

3. Stir in squash and escarole; heat to boiling over high heat. Reduce heat to low; cover and simmer 25 to 30 minutes longer or until squash and escarole are very soft.

Each serving: About 335 calories, 16g protein, 34g carbohydrate, 14g total fat (5g saturated), 9g fiber, 38mg cholesterol, 725mg sodium.

Country Borscht Stew

Originally from Russia and Poland, borscht is a soup made with fresh beets (rich in beta carotene). There are myriad versions, some of which include assorted vegetables and meat or a combination of both. Ours is so meaty, we call it stew—a perfect dish to combat winter's chill.

PREP: 1 HOUR 15 MINUTES   COOK: 2 HOURS
MAKES 16 CUPS OR 12 MAIN-DISH SERVINGS

2 bunches beets without tops
  (1 3/4 pounds)
1 medium head red cabbage (about
  2 3/4 pounds)
5 pounds beef chuck short ribs
1 pound carrots, peeled and cut
  lengthwise in half, then crosswise
  into 1-inch pieces
1 pound parsnips, peeled and cut
  lengthwise in half, then crosswise
  into 1-inch pieces

1 large onion (12 ounces), cut into
  1-inch pieces
2 teaspoons salt
1 teaspoon caraway seeds, crushed
1/4 teaspoon ground cloves
1 carton (32 ounces) chicken broth
  or 4 cups Chicken Broth (page 74)
2 bay leaves
1/2 cup loosely packed fresh dill,
  chopped
sour cream (optional)

1. Trim, peel, and shred beets (you should have about 6 1/2 cups shredded beets). Cut cabbage into quarters; remove and discard core. Cut cabbage into 1/2-inch-thick slices.

2. Heat 8-quart Dutch oven over medium-high heat until hot. Pat beef dry with paper towels. Cook beef, in batches, until well browned, about 5 to 6 minutes per batch, using slotted spoon to transfer beef to medium bowl as it is browned. (You may need to reduce heat to medium if drippings in Dutch oven begin to smoke.) Preheat oven to 325°F.

3. Reduce heat to medium. Discard all but 1/4 cup drippings in Dutch oven. Add carrots, parsnips, onion, salt, caraway seeds, and cloves; cook, stirring occasionally, until vegetables are golden, about 10 minutes. Add cabbage and cook, stirring frequently, until cabbage has wilted, about 10 minutes.

4. Return meat and any accumulated juices to Dutch oven. Add broth, bay leaves, and beets; heat to boiling over high heat, stirring until browned bits are loosened from bottom of Dutch oven. Cover and place in oven. Bake until meat is fork-tender, 2 hours to 2 hours 15 minutes.

Country Borscht Stew

5. When meat is done, transfer short ribs and bones to large bowl; cool slightly. Discard bay leaves. Skim and discard fat from liquid in Dutch oven. When short ribs are cool enough to handle, cut meat into 1-inch pieces; discard bones and fat. Return meat to Dutch oven. Heat stew over medium heat until hot; stir in dill.

6. To serve, spoon stew into shallow soup bowls and top with a dollop of sour cream, if you like.

Each serving: About 525 calories, 22g protein, 22g carbohydrate, 39g total fat (16g saturated), 82mg cholesterol, 830mg sodium.

Beef and Wheat Berry Chili

Our recipe calls for ground ancho chile pepper. Ancho chile, the dried pod of a chile indigenous to Mexico, has a sweet, fruity flavor and a mild heat. It is also called poblano when fresh. If you can't find ground ancho chile pepper in your supermarket, you can substitute Mexican-style chili powder.

PREP: ABOUT 15 MINUTES   COOK ABOUT 2 HOURS
MAKES ABOUT 8 CUPS OR 8 MAIN-DISH SERVINGS

4 teaspoons vegetable oil
2 pounds boneless beef bottom
  round, cut into 1-inch cubes
2 medium onions, chopped
3 garlic cloves, finely chopped
3 tablespoons ground ancho chile
  pepper
2 teaspoons ground cumin
Salt
1 can (14 to 14 1/2 ounces) diced
  tomatoes with chiles

1 can (14 to 14 1/2 ounces low-
  sodium beef broth or 1 3/4 cups
  Brown Beef Stock (page 116)
2 1/2 cups water
1 cup wheat berries, rinsed
1 bottle (12 ounces) dark beer
2 slices bacon
1 bay leaf
Sour cream and sliced green onions
  for garnish (optional)

1. In nonstick 5- to 6-quart Dutch oven, heat 1 teaspoon oil over medium-high heat until hot. Add half of beef and cook 4 to 5 minutes or until browned on all sides, stirring occasionally. With slotted spoon, transfer beef to large bowl. Repeat with 1 teaspoon oil and remaining beef.

2. In same Dutch oven, heat remaining 2 teaspoons oil over medium heat until hot. Add onions and cook 5 minutes or until golden, stirring occasionally. Stir in garlic and cook 30 seconds, stirring constantly. Stir in chile pepper, cumin, and 1/2 teaspoon salt; cook 1 minute. Return beef to Dutch oven; add tomatoes and broth. Heat to boiling over medium-high heat. Reduce heat to low; cover and simmer 1 1/2 hours.

3. Meanwhile, in 3-quart saucepan, combine water, wheat berries, beer, bacon, bay leaf, and 1/2 teaspoon salt; cover and heat to boiling over medium-high heat. Reduce heat to low and simmer, covered, 1 1/2 hours. Drain wheat berries, reserving 1 cup cooking water. Discard bacon and bay leaf.

4. Stir wheat berries and reserved cooking water into Dutch oven with beef mixture. Reduce heat to low and simmer, uncovered, 15 minutes or until beef and wheat berries are tender. Serve chili with sour cream and green onions if you like.

Each serving: About 360 calories, 28g protein, 23g carbohydrate, 18g total fat (6g saturated), 5g fiber, 72mg cholesterol, 530mg sodium.

Beef and Wheat Berry Chili

Chunky Chili with Beans, Slow-Cooker Style

PREP: 40 MINUTES   COOK: ABOUT 8 HOURS

MAKES ABOUT 12 CUPS OR 10 MAIN-DISH SERVINGS

4 slices bacon, cut crosswise into
   1/2–inch pieces
11/2 pounds boneless pork shoulder,
   trimmed and cut into 1-inch chunks
11/2 pound boneless beef chuck,
   trimmed and cut into 1-inch chunks
1 jumbo onion (about 1 pound),
   coarsely chopped
1/4 cup chili powder

4 large garlic cloves, crushed with
   press
1 tablespoon ground cumin
11/2 teaspoons dried oregano
Salt
1 can (28 ounces) diced tomatoes
1 cup water
3 cans (15 to 19 ounces each) pinto
   beans, rinsed and drained
Sour cream (optional)

1. In 12-inch skillet, cook bacon over medium heat until browned and crisp, stirring occasionally. With slotted spoon, transfer bacon to plate; cover and refrigerate until ready to use. Pour bacon fat into cup and reserve.

2. Increase heat to medium-high; add pork and beef in 3 batches to skillet and cook until well browned. With slotted spoon, remove meat to 5- to 6-quart slow-cooker pot as it browns.

3. Return 1 tablespoon bacon fat to skillet; reduce heat to medium. Add onion to skillet and cook 8 to 10 minutes or until tender, stirring occasionally. Stir in chili powder, garlic, cumin, oregano, and 1/2 teaspoon salt; cook 30 seconds to toast spices. Add tomatoes and water, stirring to scrape up browned bits from bottom of skillet. Remove skillet from heat.

4. To meat in slow cooker, add onion mixture and beans; stir well to combine. Cover cooker and cook chili on low setting as manufacturer directs, 8 to 10 hours (or on high setting 4 to 5 hours) or until meat is fork-tender. Skim and discard any fat from chili. Stir in bacon. Serve with sour cream if you like.

Each serving: About 400 calories, 39g protein, 31g carbohydrate, 13g total fat (4g saturated), 10g fiber, 101mg cholesterol, 875mg sodium.

Beef Burgundy

Also known as *Boeuf Bourguignon*, this French classic has become an American favorite.

PREP: ABOUT 1 HOUR   BAKE: ABOUT 1 HOUR 30 MINUTES

MAKES 10 MAIN-DISH SERVINGS

2 slices bacon, cut into 1/2-inch pieces

3 pounds boneless beef chuck, trimmed and cut into 1 1/2-inch pieces

5 medium carrots, peeled and cut into 1/2-inch pieces

3 garlic cloves, crushed with side of chef's knife

1 large onion (12 ounces), cut into 1-inch pieces

2 tablespoons all-purpose flour

2 tablespoons tomato paste

1 teaspoon salt

1/2 teaspoon coarsely ground pepper

2 cups dry red wine

4 sprigs thyme

1 package (12 ounces) mushrooms, trimmed and each cut into quarters if large

1/2 cup loosely packed fresh parsley, chopped

1. In 5- to 6-quart Dutch oven, cook bacon over medium heat until browned. With slotted spoon, transfer bacon to medium bowl.

2. Pat beef dry with paper towels. Add beef, in batches, to bacon drippings and cook over medium-high heat until well browned, using slotted spoon to transfer beef as it is browned to bowl with bacon. Preheat oven to 325°F.

3. Add carrots, garlic, and onion to Dutch oven; cook, stirring occasionally, until vegetables are browned and tender, about 10 minutes. Stir in flour, tomato paste, salt, and pepper; cook, stirring, 2 minutes. Add wine and heat to boiling, stirring until browned bits are loosened from bottom of Dutch oven.

4. Return meat, meat juices, and bacon to Dutch oven. Add thyme and mushrooms; heat to boiling. Cover and bake, stirring once, until meat is fork-tender, about 1 hour 30 minutes to 2 hours. Skim and discard fat from liquid; discard thyme sprigs. To serve, sprinkle with parsley.

Each serving: About 295 calories, 36g protein, 9g carbohydrate, 11g total fat (4g saturated), 89mg cholesterol, 375mg sodium.

Beef and Wild Mushroom Stew

To boost the meaty flavor of this stew, we've added reconstituted dried mushrooms as well as the strained soaking liquid for a richer sauce.

PREP: 30 MINUTES   COOK: 2 HOURS 15 MINUTES   MAKES 6 SERVINGS

2 tablespoons vegetable oil
1 pound mushrooms, trimmed and each cut in half
1 package (1/2 ounce) dried mushrooms
2 pounds beef for stew, cut into 11/2-inch pieces
3/4 teaspoon salt
1 large onion (12 ounces), finely chopped

2 garlic cloves, minced
2 tablespoons tomato paste
2 medium carrots, peeled and cut lengthwise in half, then crosswise into thirds
1/2 can (8 ounces) chicken broth or 1 cup Chicken Broth (page 74)
3/4 cup dry red wine
1/4 teaspoon dried thyme
1 bay leaf

1. In 5-quart Dutch oven, heat 1 tablespoon vegetable oil over medium-high heat until hot. Add fresh mushrooms and cook until tender and lightly browned and most of liquid has evaporated, about 10 minutes; transfer to small bowl.

2. Meanwhile, in small bowl, pour *1 cup boiling water* over dried mushrooms; set aside.

3. In large bowl, toss beef with salt. In same Dutch oven, heat remaining 1 tablespoon vegetable oil over medium-high heat until hot. Add half of beef and cook until browned, 10 to 12 minutes, using slotted spoon to transfer beef to bowl as it is browned. Repeat with remaining beef. Reserve drippings.

4. With slotted spoon, remove mushrooms from soaking liquid. Rinse to remove any grit, then coarsely chop. Strain liquid through sieve lined with paper towels. Set aside mushrooms and liquid.

5. Preheat oven to 350°F. Add onion and *2 tablespoons water* to drippings in Dutch oven, and cook, stirring occasionally, until onion is tender and lightly browned, about 10 minutes. Add garlic and cook 2 minutes longer. Stir in tomato paste; cook, stirring constantly, 1 minute.

6. Return beef to Dutch oven. Add dried mushrooms and their liquid, carrots, broth, red wine, thyme, and bay leaf; heat to boiling over high heat. Cover and bake 1 hour 15 minutes.

7. Add sautéed mushrooms; bake until beef is tender, about 15 minutes longer. Discard bay leaf before serving.

Each serving: About 370 calories, 36g protein, 13g carbohydrate, 18g total fat (6g saturated), 87mg cholesterol, 480mg sodium.

Braise Anatomy:
Perfect Meat in 8 Easy Steps

In the heart of winter, nothing satisfies more than a mouthwatering stew, chili, or ragout with rich succulent meat. Follow these steps for no-fail browning and braising:

- Choose a heavy-bottomed Dutch oven or skillet for best browning. Make sure it has a tight-fitting lid to keep in steam when simmering.
- Pat meat dry with paper towels to remove excess moisture.
- Season meat just before cooking to help prevent it from releasing its natural juices.
- Add meat in small batches (a pound or less at a time) to hot oil over high heat. Do not overcrowd the pan. It will cause meat to steam instead of allowing it to brown.
- Be patient: Allow meat to turn deep brown on all sides, caramelizing the proteins and sugars. (You may need to reduce heat if bottom of pan becomes too dark.)
- Add liquid to meat in pan and heat to boiling, scraping bottom of pan with spoon to release browned bits.
- Cover pan and braise mixture over low heat on top of range or place in oven at moderate temperature (325 degrees to 350 degrees F) to cook. Do not allow mixture to boil—it will toughen and dry out the meat.
- Check for doneness: When meat is tender, a fork will slip easily in and out of it.

Overnight Beef Stew

This hearty beef-and-vegetable medley will be waiting for you at home at the end of the day; all you have to do before serving is thicken the cooking broth. For a stress-free morning, prep the ingredients the night before.

PREP: 25 MINUTES   COOK: 8 TO 10 HOURS   MAKES 12 SERVINGS

3 large stalks celery, cut into
    1/2-inch-thick slices
1 large onion (12 ounces), cut into
    16 wedges
1 bag (16 ounces) peeled baby
    carrots
2 tablespoons ground coriander
1 tablespoon ground ginger
1 teaspoon salt
1/4 teaspoon ground nutmeg

1/4 teaspoon dried thyme
1/4 teaspoon coarsely ground black
    pepper
4 pounds boneless beef chuck for
    stew, cut into 2-inch pieces
1 can (14 1/2 ounces) stewed
    tomatoes
3 tablespoons all-purpose flour
1/4 cup water

1. Mix celery, onion, and carrots in bottom of 5 1/2- to 6 1/2-quart slow-cooker pot. In large bowl, combine coriander, ginger, salt, nutmeg, thyme, and pepper; add beef and toss until evenly coated. Transfer beef mixture to pot with vegetables. Pour stewed tomatoes over beef. (It's not necessary to stir.) Cover pot with lid and cook on Low setting as manufacturer directs until beef is fork-tender, 8 to 10 hours.

2. When beef is tender and ready to serve, strain stew over 3-quart saucepan; return beef and vegetables to slow-cooker pot. Skim and discard fat from liquid in saucepan. Heat liquid to boiling over high heat.

3. Meanwhile, in cup, with fork, mix flour and water until smooth. Gradually whisk flour mixture into liquid; heat to boiling. Boil, stirring occasionally, until gravy thickens slightly, about 1 minute. Pour gravy over beef and vegetables in pot.

Each serving: About 325 calories, 39g protein, 12g carbohydrate, 13g total fat (5g saturated), 91mg cholesterol, 425mg sodium.

Overnight Beef Stew

Beef Stew with Red Wine

Beef Stew with Red Wine

Using store-bought precooked beef roast au jus and fresh precut vegetables makes this hearty stew a snap to prepare. It's perfect for those evenings when time is limited.

PREP: 5 MINUTES   COOK: ABOUT 20 MINUTES
MAKES ABOUT 6 CUPS OR 4 MAIN-DISH SERVINGS

1 pound red potatoes (about 4
   medium), cut into 1-inch pieces
2 teaspoons vegetable oil
2 large garlic cloves, sliced
1 medium onion, cut into 1-inch
   pieces
1 bag (10 ounces) stringless snap
   pea and carrot blend

1/4 cup water
1/2 cup dry red wine
1 package (17 ounces) fully cooked
   beef roast au jus, cut into 1-inch
   pieces and juices reserved
1/8 teaspoon ground black pepper

1. Place potatoes in microwave-safe pie plate or medium bowl. Cook in microwave oven on High until fork-tender, about 4 minutes.
2. Meanwhile, in 12-inch skillet, heat oil over medium heat until hot. Add garlic and onion and cook until tender and lightly browned, about 5 minutes. Add snap peas and carrots and water; cover and cook, stirring occasionally, until carrots are tender, 5 to 6 minutes.
3. Add wine to skillet; boil 1 minute. Stir in beef with its juices and pepper and cook until heated through, about 2 minutes. Gently stir in potatoes just before serving.

Each serving: About 340 calories, 28g protein, 35g carbohydrate, 10g total fat (4g saturated), 64mg cholesterol, 415mg sodium.

Slow-Cooker Short Ribs with Root Vegetables

A slow-cooker makes preparing dinner as easy as prep it and forget it!

PREP: 35 MINUTES   COOK: 8 TO 10 HOURS
MAKES 6 MAIN-DISH SERVINGS

3 pounds bone-in beef chuck short ribs

salt and ground black pepper

2 large parsnips (about 4 ounces each), peeled and cut into 1-inch pieces

1 medium turnip (about 8 ounces), peeled and cut into 1-inch pieces

1 bag (16 ounces) peeled baby carrots

1 jumbo onion (about 1 pound), coarsely chopped

4 large garlic cloves, thinly sliced

1 teaspoon dried thyme

2 cups dry red wine

1/4 cup tomato paste

1. Heat 12-inch skillet over medium-high heat until hot. Add ribs to skillet and sprinkle with 1/2 teaspoon salt and 1/4 teaspoon pepper. Cook ribs, turning occasionally, until well browned, about 10 minutes.

2. Meanwhile, in 5- to 6-quart slow-cooker pot, place parsnips, turnip, and carrots.

3. Transfer ribs to slow-cooker, placing them on top of vegetables. Discard drippings from skillet. Reduce heat to medium; add onion to skillet and cook, stirring frequently, until browned, about 8 minutes. Stir in garlic and thyme and cook, stirring constantly, 1 minute. Add wine and heat to boiling over high heat, stirring to loosen browned bits from bottom of skillet.

4. Remove from heat and stir in tomato paste, 1/2 teaspoon salt, and 1/4 teaspoon pepper; pour over ribs in slow-cooker. Cover slow-cooker and cook on Low setting as manufacturer directs, until meat is fork-tender and falling off the bones, 8 to 10 hours (or on High setting 4 to 5 hours).

5. With tongs, transfer ribs to deep platter; discard bones, if you like. Skim and discard fat from sauce in slow-cooker. Spoon vegetables and sauce over ribs.

Each serving: About 655 calories, 27g protein, 24g carbohydrate, 50g total fat (21g saturated), 114mg cholesterol, 535mg sodium.

Chinese-Spiced Beef Stew

Our beef stew with broccoli and snow peas in a flavorful broth accented with ginger and star anise.

PREP: 20 MINUTES   COOK: 2 HOURS TO 2 HOURS 30 MINUTES
MAKES 8 MAIN-DISH SERVINGS

2 pounds boneless beef chuck, cut
  into 1¹/₂-inch pieces
2 tablespoons vegetable oil
¹/₃ cup dry sherry
2 tablespoons sugar
3 tablespoons soy sauce
1 piece fresh ginger (3" by 1"),
  peeled and thinly sliced
2 garlic cloves, peeled

2 whole star anise
4 strips (3" by 1" each) orange peel
3 cups water
1 bunch broccoli (1¹/₂ pounds), cut
  into 1¹/₂" by 1" pieces
4 ounces snow peas, trimmed
1 bunch green onions, trimmed and
  cut into 2-inch pieces

1. Pat beef dry with paper towels. In 5-quart Dutch oven, heat 1 table-spoon vegetable oil over medium-high heat until hot. Add half of beef and cook until well browned, using slotted spoon to transfer beef to plate as it is browned. Repeat with remaining 1 tablespoon oil and beef.
2. Return beef to Dutch oven. Add sherry, sugar, soy sauce, ginger, garlic, star anise, orange peel, and water; heat to boiling over high heat. Reduce heat to low; cover and simmer until meat is fork-tender, 1 hour to 1 hour 15 minutes.
3. With slotted spoon, transfer meat to serving bowl and keep warm. Discard star anise. Increase heat to high and boil liquid until reduced to 2 cups, about 15 minutes. Skim and discard fat from broth.
4. Meanwhile, in 4-quart saucepan, heat *1 inch water* to boiling over high heat. Add broccoli. Reduce heat to low; cover and simmer 5 minutes. Add snow peas and green onions and cook, covered, until all vegetables are tender-crisp, about 3 minutes longer. Drain vegetables and add beef to vegetable mixture. Pour reduced broth on top.

Each serving: About 370 calories, 27g protein, 12g carbohydrate, 24g total fat (8g saturated), 85mg cholesterol, 460mg sodium.

Spanish Beef Stew

Unlike most stews, this begins with a whole piece of meat, which is shredded after cooking. In Spanish, it is called *Ropa Vieja* because the shredded meat resembles old rags.

PREP: 45 MINUTES   COOK: 3 HOURS 30 MINUTES TO 4 HOURS
MAKES 6 MAIN-DISH SERVINGS

1 beef flank steak (about
  1 3/4 pounds)
1 medium onion, coarsely chopped
1 medium carrot, peeled and coarsely
  chopped
1 bay leaf
2 teaspoons salt
5 cups water
4 teaspoons olive oil
1 large onion (12 ounces), sliced
1 red pepper, cut into 1/2-inch-wide
  strips

1 yellow pepper, cut into 1/2-inch-
  wide strips
1 green pepper, cut into 1/2-inch-wide
  strips
3 garlic cloves, crushed with garlic
  press
3 serrano or jalapeño chiles, seeded
  and minced
1/4 teaspoon ground cinnamon
1 can (14 1/2 to 16 ounces) stewed
  tomatoes
capers, rinsed and drained

1. Cut flank steak into thirds; place in 5-quart Dutch oven. Add chopped onion, carrot, bay leaf, 1 teaspoon salt, and water and heat to boiling over high heat. Reduce heat to low; cover and simmer until meat is very tender, 2 hours 30 minutes to 3 hours. Remove from heat and let steak stand, uncovered, 30 minutes. (Or, cover and refrigerate overnight.)

2. In 12-inch skillet, heat oil over medium-high heat until hot. Add sliced onion; red, yellow, and green peppers; and remaining 1 teaspoon salt and cook, stirring often, until vegetables are tender, about 15 minutes. Stir in garlic, serranos, and cinnamon and cook 30 seconds. Stir in tomatoes with their juice; cook 5 minutes.

3. With slotted spoon, transfer beef to large bowl; strain broth. Skim and discard fat from broth. Reserve 2 cups broth. (Reserve remaining broth for another use.) With two forks, shred beef into fine strips.

4. Stir 2 cups reserved broth and shredded meat into pepper mixture and simmer, uncovered, 10 minutes, stirring occasionally. To serve, sprinkle with capers.

Each serving: About 350 calories, 38g protein, 10g carbohydrate, 17g total fat (7g saturated), 65mg cholesterol, 720mg sodium.

Spanish Beef Stew

Scandinavian Beef Stew

Root vegetables and chunks of beef are cooked until tender in a broth spiced with ginger, nutmeg, and coriander.

PREP: 30 MINUTES   COOK: 2 HOURS TO 2 HOURS 15 MINUTES
MAKES 8 MAIN-DISH SERVINGS

2 pounds boneless beef chuck, cut
   into 1¹/₂-inch pieces
2 tablespoons vegetable oil
1 medium onion, finely chopped
2 tablespoons ground ginger
1 tablespoon ground coriander
¹/₄ teaspoon ground nutmeg
1 can (14 to 14¹/₂ ounces) beef
   broth, or 1³/₄ cups Brown Beef
   Stock (page 116)
1 teaspoon salt
¹/₄ teaspoon coarsely ground black
   pepper

¹/₄ teaspoon dried thyme
1 bag (16 ounces) carrots, peeled
   and cut into 1¹/₂-inch pieces
2 large parsnips (8 ounces), peeled
   and cut into 1¹/₂-inch pieces
¹/₂ small rutabaga, peeled and cut
   into 1-inch pieces (1¹/₂ cups)
1 pound small red potatoes, each cut
   in half
2 tablespoons chopped fresh parsley

1. Pat beef dry with paper towels. In 5-quart Dutch oven, heat 1 tablespoon oil over medium-high heat until hot. Add half of beef and cook until well browned, using slotted spoon to transfer beef to plate as it is browned. Repeat with remaining 1 tablespoon oil and beef.

2. Reduce heat to medium; add onion and cook until tender, about 10 minutes. Stir in ginger, coriander, and nutmeg and cook 30 seconds. Add enough *water* to broth to equal 3 cups. Return beef to Dutch oven; stir in broth mixture, salt, pepper, and thyme; heat to boiling over high heat. Reduce heat to low; cover and simmer until meat is almost fork-tender, 1 hour to 1 hour 15 minutes.

3. Skim and discard fat from liquid in Dutch oven. Add carrots, parsnips, rutabaga, and potatoes; heat to boiling over high heat. Reduce heat to low; cover and simmer until vegetables and meat are tender, about 30 minutes longer. To serve, sprinkle with parsley.

Each serving: About 420 calories, 27g protein, 25g carbohydrate, 24g total fat (8g saturated), 85mg cholesterol, 515mg sodium.

Chili

For extra fire, use hot Mexican chili powder.

PREP: 15 MINUTES   COOK: 3 HOURS   MAKES 6 MAIN-DISH SERVINGS

2 pounds lean boneless beef chuck, trimmed and cut into 1-inch pieces
1 tablespoon olive oil
1 large onion (12 ounces), chopped
1 large green pepper, cut into 1-inch pieces
3 garlic cloves, finely chopped
2 tablespoons chili powder

1 teaspoon ground cumin
1 teaspoon ground coriander
1/2 teaspoon dried oregano, crumbled
1/2 teaspoon salt
1 can (28 ounces) plum tomatoes in puree, chopped
1 can (15 to 19 ounces) red kidney beans, rinsed and drained

1. Pat beef dry with paper towels. In nonreactive 5-quart Dutch oven, heat oil over medium heat until very hot. Add half of beef and cook until browned, using slotted spoon to transfer meat to bowl as it is browned. Repeat with remaining beef.

2. Add onion, green pepper, and garlic to Dutch oven and cook, stirring occasionally, until onion is tender, about 5 minutes. Stir in chili powder, cumin, coriander, oregano, and salt; cook 1 minute. Add tomatoes with their puree and heat to boiling. Reduce heat; cover and simmer until meat is tender, about 2 hours 30 minutes.

3. Add beans and cook, stirring occasionally, until heated through, about 15 minutes longer. Before serving, skim and discard fat from chili liquid.

Each serving: About 368 calories, 36g protein, 24g carbohydrate, 15g total fat (5g saturated), 98mg cholesterol, 647mg sodium.

Latin-Style Braised Beef

Garlic and oregano plus the zing of fresh citrus juice give this stew the traditional flavors of the cuisines of Puerto Rico, Cuba, and Central America.

PREP: 40 MINUTES   COOK: 3 HOURS 15 MINUTES
MAKES ABOUT 7 CUPS OR 6 MAIN-DISH SERVINGS

1 beef flank steak (about 1 1/2 pounds), well trimmed
2 large oranges
2 medium carrots
2 large onions (about 1 1/2 pounds)
1 bay leaf
1 teaspoon salt
3 cups water
2 tablespoons olive oil
2 red peppers, cut into 1/2-inch-wide strips
2 yellow peppers, cut into 1/2-inch-wide strips
4 garlic cloves, crushed with garlic press
2 jalapeño chiles, seeded and minced
1/2 teaspoon dried oregano
2 tablespoons fresh lime juice
chopped fresh cilantro and lime wedges for garnish

1. Cut flank steak in half, then cut each half crosswise into thirds. Place steak in 8-quart Dutch oven. From oranges, remove 2 strips peel, 3" by 1" each, and squeeze 1/2 cup juice. Coarsely chop carrots and 1 onion. Add orange-peel strips, chopped carrots and onion, bay leaf, salt, and water to Dutch oven; heat to boiling over high heat. Reduce heat to low; cover and simmer until meat is very tender, about 2 hours 30 minutes.

2. With slotted spoon, transfer meat to large bowl. Strain broth through sieve into medium bowl, pressing on vegetables with back of spoon to extract as much as broth as possible; discard vegetables. Rinse and dry Dutch oven.

3. Slice remaining onion. In Dutch oven, heat oil over medium-high heat until hot. Add red and yellow peppers and sliced onion and cook, stirring occasionally, until vegetables are tender and golden, about 25 minutes.

4. Meanwhile, with two forks, shred beef into fine strips.

5. Stir garlic, chiles, and oregano into pepper mixture; cook, stirring, 2 minutes longer.

6. Skim and discard fat from reserved broth. Add broth, shredded meat, orange juice, and lime juice to Dutch oven; heat to boiling. Reduce heat to medium and simmer, uncovered, until heated through, about 10 minutes. Sprinkle with cilantro and serve with lime wedges.

Each serving: About 265 calories, 23g protein, 17g carbohydrate, 12g total fat (4g saturated), 39mg cholesterol, 460mg sodium.

Latin-Style Braised Beef

Salsa Beef Stew

Salsa Beef Stew

We used a jar of mild salsa to add Tex-Mex pizazz to this chili-like entrée and substituted ground beef for cubes of meat to speed up the cooking. Accompany with crunchy tortilla chips.

PREP: 10 MINUTES   COOK: 25 MINUTES
MAKES ABOUT 10 CUPS OR 8 MAIN-DISH SERVINGS

1 1/2 pounds lean ground beef
1 large onion (12 ounces), chopped
3 tablespoons chili powder
1 tablespoon olive oil
1 carrot, peeled and chopped
1 jar (16 ounces) mild salsa
1 can (14 to 14 1/2 ounces) chicken broth, or 1 3/4 cups Chicken Broth (page 74)

1 can (15 to 19 ounces) no-salt-added black beans, rinsed and drained
1 can (11 ounces) no-salt-added whole-kernel corn, drained
1 can (14 1/2 ounces) diced tomatoes in puree
1/2 cup loosely packed fresh cilantro

1. Heat nonstick 12-inch skillet over medium-high heat until very hot but not smoking. Add ground beef and half of onion and cook, stirring occasionally to break up beef, until liquid has evaporated and beef is browned, about 8 minutes. Stir in chili powder and cook 2 minutes.

2. Meanwhile, in 5- to 6-quart Dutch oven, heat oil over medium-high heat until hot. Add carrot and remaining onion, and cook, stirring occasionally, until golden, about 5 minutes. Stir in salsa, broth, beans, corn, and tomatoes with their juice; cook, stirring occasionally, 5 minutes.

3. Stir beef mixture into bean mixture; heat through. To serve, sprinkle with cilantro.

Each serving: About 415 calories, 23g protein, 35g carbohydrate, 21g total fat (8g saturated), 64mg cholesterol, 940mg sodium.

Roasted Chile and Tomatillo Stew

Roasted Chile and Tomatillo Stew

The tomatillo, sometimes called a Mexican green tomato, has a papery husk that should be removed before using.

PREP: 1 HOUR   COOK: 2 HOURS 45 MINUTES TO 3 HOURS 15 MINUTES
MAKES 8 MAIN-DISH SERVINGS

4 poblano chiles or 2 green peppers
1 bunch cilantro
3 garlic cloves
1 1/2 teaspoons salt
2 pounds boneless pork shoulder, trimmed and cut into 3/4-inch pieces
2 medium onions, finely chopped
3 serrano or jalapeño chiles, seeded and minced

1 teaspoon ground cumin
1/4 teaspoon ground red pepper (cayenne)
2 pounds tomatillos, husked, washed well, and each cut into quarters
1 can (15 1/4 to 16 ounces) whole-kernel corn, drained
warm flour tortillas (optional)

1. Preheat broiler. Line broiling pan with foil. Cut poblanos or green peppers lengthwise in half; remove and discard stem and seeds. Arrange peppers, cut side down, in prepared broiling pan. Place pan in broiler, 5 to 6 inches from heat source. Broil, without turning, until skin is charred and blistered, 15 minutes. Wrap poblanos in foil and allow to steam at room temperature until cool enough to handle. Remove peppers from foil. Peel skin and discard. Cut into 1-inch pieces.

2. Turn oven control to 325°F. Chop enough cilantro leaves and stems to measure 1/4 cup; chop and reserve another 1/4 cup cilantro leaves for garnish. On cutting board, mash garlic and salt into a paste. Transfer garlic mixture to heavy 5-quart Dutch oven. Add cilantro leaves and stems, pork, onions, chiles, cumin, and ground red pepper; toss to combine. Cover and bake 1 hour.

3. Stir in tomatillos and roasted poblanos. Cover and bake until meat is very tender, 1 hour 30 minutes to 2 hours.

4. Skim and discard fat from liquid in Dutch oven. Stir in corn and heat through. Sprinkle with reserved cilantro and serve with tortillas, if you like.

Each serving without tortillas: About 370 calories, 23g protein, 20g carbohydrate, 23g total fat (8g saturated), 67mg cholesterol, 600mg sodium.

Hungarian Goulash

This well-known stew, seasoned with sweet paprika, can be made with beef, lamb, veal, or chicken. It became popular in the Midwest, where many Hungarian immigrants settled to farm. Its Hungarian name, *gulyás,* once meant "herdsman" but has since become synonymous with this popular recipe. It is usually served over hot, buttered noodles.

PREP: 30 MINUTES   COOK: ABOUT 1 HOUR 15 MINUTES
MAKES ABOUT 6 CUPS OR 6 MAIN-DISH SERVINGS

2 pounds veal shoulder chops, meat removed from bone, trimmed, and cut into 1-inch pieces
2 tablespoons olive oil
2 large onions (about 1 1/2 pounds), each cut in half and thinly sliced
1 garlic clove, crushed with garlic press

3 tablespoons sweet paprika
1 can (14 to 14 1/2 ounces) stewed tomatoes
1/2 teaspoon salt
3/4 cup water
1/2 cup reduced-fat sour cream
hot cooked egg noodles

1. Pat veal dry with paper towels. In nonstick 5- or 6-quart Dutch oven, heat 1 1/2 teaspoons oil over medium-high heat until hot. Add half of veal and cook until browned, using slotted spoon to transfer veal to bowl as it is browned. Repeat with 1 1/2 teaspoons oil and remaining veal; set aside.

2. Add remaining 1 tablespoon oil and heat over medium heat until hot. Add onions, garlic, and paprika and cook, stirring occasionally, until onions are tender, about 15 minutes.

3. Return veal to pot. Add stewed tomatoes, salt, and water; heat to boiling over medium-high heat. Reduce heat to low; cover and simmer, stirring occasionally, until meat is fork-tender, about 1 hour 15 minutes.

4. Stir in sour cream and heat through but do *not* boil. To serve, spoon goulash over hot egg noodles.

Each serving without noodles: About 245 calories, 27g protein, 12g carbohydrate, 10g total fat (3g saturated), 108mg cholesterol, 460mg sodium.

Hungarian Pork Goulash

In this version, we've added sauerkraut to the traditionally lavish amounts of onions and paprika.

PREP: 20 MINUTES   COOK: 1 HOUR 50 MINUTES
MAKES 6 MAIN-DISH SERVINGS

2 tablespoons vegetable oil
2 large onions (about 1 1/2 pounds), chopped
1 garlic clove, minced
1/4 cup paprika
2 pounds boneless pork shoulder blade roast (fresh pork butt), cut into 1 1/2-inch pieces
1 package (16 ounces) sauerkraut, rinsed and drained

1 can (14 to 14 1/2 ounces) diced tomatoes
1 can (14 to 14 1/2 ounces) beef broth, or 1 3/4 cups Brown Beef Stock (page 116)
1/2 teaspoon salt
1/4 teaspoon ground black pepper
1 container (8 ounces) light sour cream
hot cooked egg noodles (optional)

1. In 5-quart Dutch oven or saucepot, heat oil over medium heat until hot. Add onions; cook 10 minutes. Stir in garlic; cook, stirring often, until onions are very tender, about 5 minutes longer.

2. Preheat oven to 325°F. Stir in paprika; cook 1 minute. Add pork, sauerkraut, tomatoes with their juice, broth, salt, and pepper; heat to boiling over high heat. Cover and bake until meat is fork-tender, 1 hour 30 minutes.

3. Remove stew from oven and let stand for 10 minutes. Stir in sour cream. Heat through on top of range over medium heat (do not boil). Serve over noodles, if you like.

Each serving without noodles: About 525 calories, 31g protein, 15g carbohydrate, 39g total fat (14g saturated), 104mg cholesterol, 920mg sodium.

Pork and Posole Stew

Posole is usually made with hominy—dried white or yellow corn kernels with the hull and germ removed. Our version uses canned hominy, which has already been reconstituted.

PREP: 45 MINUTES   COOK: 2 HOURS

MAKES ABOUT 10 CUPS OR 10 MAIN-DISH SERVINGS

2 medium red peppers
3 pounds boneless pork shoulder, well trimmed and cut into 1 1/2-inch pieces
1 jumbo onion (1 pound), chopped
4 garlic cloves, minced
3 jalapeño chiles, seeded and minced
1 cup loosely packed fresh cilantro leaves and stems, chopped
2 teaspoons ground cumin

1 1/2 teaspoons salt
1/2 teaspoon dried oregano
1/4 teaspoon ground red pepper (cayenne)
1 cup water
1 can (29 ounces) hominy, rinsed and drained
lime wedges, radishes, and chopped cilantro

1. Preheat broiler. Line broiling pan (without rack) with foil. Cut each red pepper lengthwise in half; remove and discard stem and seeds. Arrange peppers, cut side down, in prepared broiling pan. Place pan in broiler 5 to 6 inches from heat source. Broil until skin is charred and blistered, 8 to 10 minutes. Wrap peppers in foil and allow to steam at room temperature until cool enough to handle, about 15 minutes. Turn oven to 325°F.

2. Remove peppers from foil; peel off skin and discard. Cut peppers into 1-inch pieces.

3. In 5-quart Dutch oven, combine roasted peppers, pork, onion, garlic, jalapeños, cilantro, cumin, salt, oregano, and ground red pepper. Stir in water; heat to boiling over high heat. Cover and bake until pork is very tender, about 1 hour 30 minutes.

4. Remove from oven; skim and discard fat. Stir in hominy; cover and bake until heated through, about 15 minutes longer. Garnish with lime wedges, radishes, and chopped cilantro.

Each serving: About 300 calories, 38g protein, 14g carbohydrate, 9g total fat (3g saturated), 83mg cholesterol, 565mg sodium.

Pork and Posole Stew

Rustic Lamb Stew

Rustic Lamb Stew

A rich alternative to a typical beef stew.

PREP: 75 MINUTES   COOK: ABOUT 1 HOUR 30 MINUTES
MAKES ABOUT 14 1/2 CUPS OR 12 MAIN-DISH SERVINGS

5 pounds boneless lamb shoulder or boneless beef chuck, trimmed and cut into 2-inch pieces
2 teaspoons plus 1 tablespoon vegetable oil
6 garlic cloves, sliced
2 pounds carrots, peeled and cut into 1-inch pieces
2 medium onions, cut into 1-inch pieces
1/4 cup all-purpose flour
2 teaspoons salt

1 teaspoon ground allspice
1/2 teaspoon ground black pepper
1/4 cup tomato paste
1 cup dry white wine
10 thyme sprigs
1 can (14 to 14 1/2 ounces) chicken broth, or 1 3/4 cups Chicken Broth (page 74)
1 bag (16 ounces) frozen peas
crusty bread (optional)

1. Pat lamb dry with paper towels. In 6- to 8-quart Dutch oven, heat 2 teaspoons oil over medium-high heat until hot. Add lamb, in batches, and cook until well browned on all sides, 6 to 8 minutes, adding more oil if necessary, and using a slotted spoon, transfer lamb to medium bowl as it is browned. (You may need to reduce heat to medium if oil in Dutch oven begins to smoke.) Preheat oven to 325°F.

2. Reduce heat to medium. In same Dutch oven, heat remaining 1 tablespoon oil. Add garlic, carrots, and onions and cook, stirring occasionally, until vegetables are browned and tender, about 10 minutes. Stir in flour, salt, allspice, and pepper; cook 2 minutes. Add tomato paste, then wine, and heat to boiling, stirring until browned bits are loosened from bottom of Dutch oven; boil 5 minutes. Return lamb with its juices to Dutch oven. Stir in thyme sprigs and broth; heat to boiling.

3. Cover and bake until meat is fork-tender, about 1 hour 30 minutes. Skim and discard fat from liquid; remove and discard thyme sprigs. Stir in frozen peas; heat through. Serve with crusty bread, if you like.

Each serving without bread: About 520 calories, 48g protein, 18g carbohydrate, 27g total fat (9g saturated), 155mg cholesterol, 715mg sodium.

Lamb Shanks with White Beans and Roasted Endive

Perfect for a winter dinner with friends, this bistro classic just needs a crisp green salad and some hearty red wine, like a Cabernet or Shiraz to round out the meal.

PREP: ABOUT 1 HOUR 30 MINUTES   BAKE: ABOUT 2 HOURS
MAKES 8 MAIN-DISH SERVINGS

WHITE BEANS AND LAMB SHANKS
1 package (16 ounces) dry Great Northern beans, rinsed and picked through
8 small lamb shanks (about 1 pound each)
2 1/2 teaspoons salt
1 teaspoon coarsely ground pepper
2 tablespoons vegetable oil
6 medium garlic cloves, crushed with side of chef's knife
4 carrots, each cut crosswise into 1-inch pieces
1 large onion (12 ounces), coarsely chopped
1/4 cup all-purpose flour

2 tablespoons tomato paste
2 cups dry white wine
1 can (14 to 14 1/2 ounces) chicken broth, or 1 3/4 cups Chicken Broth (page 74)
1 cup water
2 sprigs rosemary plus 8 sprigs for garnish

ROASTED ENDIVE
1 tablespoon olive oil
1/2 teaspoon salt
1/4 teaspoon coarsely ground pepper
8 medium heads Belgian endive (about 1 1/2 pounds)

1. Prepare White Beans: In 4-quart saucepan, heat beans and enough *water to cover by 2 inches* to boiling over high heat. Remove saucepan from heat and set aside until beans have softened, about 40 minutes. Drain. (Or, if you prefer, soak beans overnight in cold water; drain.)

2. Meanwhile, prepare Lamb Shanks: Pat lamb dry with paper towels; sprinkle with 1 teaspoon salt and 1/2 teaspoon pepper. In 8-quart Dutch oven, heat oil over medium-high heat until very hot but not smoking. Cook shanks in batches until browned all sides, 12 to 15 minutes, using slotted spoon to transfer shanks to large bowl as they are browned. If necessary, reduce heat to medium before adding second batch of shanks to prevent overbrowning.

3. Preheat oven to 375°F. Add garlic, carrots, and onion to Dutch oven; cook, stirring frequently, until browned and tender, about 10 minutes. Add flour, tomato paste, and remaining 1 1/2 teaspoons salt and 1/2 teaspoon pepper; cook, stirring constantly, 2 minutes. Add wine and heat to boiling, stirring until browned bits are loosened from bottom of pot; boil 5 minutes. Add broth and water; heat to boiling. Stir in cooked beans and 2 sprigs rosemary. Return shanks to pot and heat to boiling. Cover and bake 1 hour.

4. Meanwhile, prepare Roasted Endive: In large bowl, with fork, mix oil, salt, and pepper. Trim root ends from endive and cut each lengthwise in half. Toss endive with oil mixture until evenly coated. In 15 1/2" by 10 1/2" jelly-roll pan, arrange endive, cut sides down.

5. After 1 hour, turn shanks and replace cover. Place endive and shanks in same oven. Bake shanks and endive until meat is fork-tender and easily separates from bone and endive is very tender and bottoms begin to brown, about 1 hour.

6. With slotted spoon, transfer shanks to large bowl. Skim and discard fat from liquid in pot. Remove and discard rosemary.

7. To serve, divide beans and cooking liquid equally among 8 large dinner plates; top each with a lamb shank and 2 endive halves. Garnish with a rosemary sprig.

Each serving lamb and beans: About 725 calories, 67g protein, 46g carbohydrate, 28g total fat (11g saturated), 198mg cholesterol, 1,110mg sodium.

Each serving endive: About 30 calories, 1g protein, 3g carbohydrate, 2g total fat (0g saturated), 0mg cholesterol, 145mg sodium.

Greek-Style Lamb Shanks

A savory stew that combines four classic Greek flavors: lemon, dill, parsley, and lamb.

PREP: 30 MINUTES   BAKE: 2 HOURS 45 MINUTES
MAKES 4 MAIN-DISH SERVINGS

4 small lamb shanks (1 pound each)
1 teaspoon salt
1 tablespoon vegetable oil
2 medium onions, cut into 1/2-inch pieces
1 large carrot, cut into 1/2-inch pieces
2 garlic cloves, minced
1 can (14 to 14 1/2 ounces) diced tomatoes
1/2 can (8 ounces) chicken broth or 1 cup Chicken Broth (page 74)

4 medium all-purpose potatoes (about 1 3/4 pounds), each cut into quarters
3/4 pound green beans, cut into 2-inch pieces
2 medium lemons
2 tablespoons chopped fresh dill
2 tablespoons chopped fresh parsley

1. Pat lamb dry with paper towels; sprinkle with 1/4 teaspoon salt. In 8-quart Dutch oven, heat oil over medium-high heat until hot. Cook lamb shanks, two at a time, until browned, using slotted spoon to transfer shanks to bowl as they are browned.

2. Preheat oven to 350°F. To drippings in Dutch oven, add onions and carrot and cook until tender and lightly browned, about 10 minutes. Add garlic; cook 2 minutes.

3. Return lamb shanks to Dutch oven. Add tomatoes with their juice, chicken broth, and remaining 3/4 teaspoon salt; heat to boiling over high heat. Cover and bake 1 hour 30 minutes. Turn lamb shanks. Add potatoes and green beans; cover and bake until lamb and potatoes are fork-tender, about 1 hour 15 minutes.

4. Meanwhile, from lemons, grate 1 tablespoon peel and squeeze 2 tablespoons juice.

5. When lamb shanks are done, skim fat from sauce and discard. Stir in lemon peel, lemon juice, dill, and parsley.

Each serving: About 625 calories, 50g protein, 53g carbohydrate, 24g total fat (9g saturated), 159mg cholesterol, 995mg sodium.

Veal Stew with Orange Gremolata

A baked stew made with onion, carrots, and tomatoes. Just before serving, stir in gremolata, a flavorful garnish of garlic, parsley, and grated citrus peel.

PREP: 20 MINUTES   BAKE: 1 HOUR 15 MINUTES
MAKES 6 MAIN-DISH SERVINGS

2 pounds boneless veal shoulder, trimmed and cut into 1½-inch pieces
2 tablespoons vegetable oil
4 medium carrots, cut into 2-inch pieces
1 medium onion, chopped
½ can (8 ounces) chicken broth or 1 cup Chicken Broth (page 74)

1 can (16 ounces) tomatoes in puree
¾ teaspoon salt
¼ teaspoon coarsely ground black pepper
¼ teaspoon dried thyme
2 garlic cloves, minced
2 tablespoons chopped fresh parsley
1 tablespoon grated orange peel

1. Preheat oven to 350°F. Pat veal dry with paper towels. In 5-quart Dutch oven, heat 1 tablespoon oil over medium-high heat until hot. Add half of veal and cook until browned, using slotted spoon to transfer meat to bowl as it is browned. Repeat with remaining veal.

2. In same Dutch oven, heat remaining 1 tablespoon oil over medium heat until hot. Add carrots and onions and cook until browned, about 10 minutes.

3. Add broth, stirring until brown bits are loosened from bottom of pot. Return veal to Dutch oven. Add tomatoes with their puree, salt, pepper, and thyme and heat to boiling over high heat. Cover and bake until meat and vegetables are tender, about 1 hour 15 minutes.

4. In small bowl, with fork, mix garlic, parsley, and grated orange peel; stir into stew just before serving.

Each serving: About 305 calories, 31g protein, 11g carbohydrate, 15g total fat (5g saturated), 126mg cholesterol, 640mg sodium.

Moroccan Lamb with Couscous

In authentic Moroccan cooking, the term *couscous* refers to the entire dish, not just the pasta, as it does here.

PREP: 20 MINUTES   COOK: 1 HOUR 45 MINUTES
MAKES 8 MAIN-DISH SERVINGS

2 pounds boneless lamb shoulder, trimmed and cut into 1 1/4-inch pieces
2 tablespoons olive oil
2 garlic cloves, minced
1 1/2 teaspoons ground cumin
1 1/2 teaspoons ground coriander
1 large onion (12 ounces), cut into 8 wedges
1 can (14 1/2 to 16 ounces) stewed tomatoes
1 cinnamon stick (3 inches)
1 1/4 teaspoons salt
1/4 teaspoon ground red pepper (cayenne)
1 cup water
3 large sweet potatoes (about 2 pounds), peeled and cut into 2-inch pieces
1 cup dark seedless raisins
1 can (15 to 19 ounces) garbanzo beans, rinsed and drained
2 cups couscous
1/4 cup chopped fresh cilantro

1. Pat lamb dry with paper towels. In 5-quart Dutch oven, heat 1 tablespoon oil over medium-high heat until hot. Add half of lamb and cook until browned, using slotted spoon to transfer meat to bowl as it is browned. Repeat with remaining 1 tablespoon oil and lamb.

2. To drippings in Dutch oven, add garlic, cumin, and coriander; cook 30 seconds. Return lamb to Dutch oven. Stir in onion, stewed tomatoes, cinnamon stick, salt, ground red pepper, and water; heat to boiling over high heat. Reduce heat to low; cover and simmer, stirring occasionally, 45 minutes.

3. Stir in sweet potatoes; cook, covered, until lamb and vegetables are fork-tender, about 30 minutes longer.

4. Stir in raisins and beans; cook, covered, until heated through, about 5 minutes longer.

5. Meanwhile, prepare couscous as label directs. Stir in 1 tablespoon cilantro.

6. Just before serving, stir in remaining cilantro. Serve stew with couscous.

Each serving: About 750 calories, 33g protein, 87g carbohydrate, 30g total fat (11g saturated), 90mg cholesterol, 720mg sodium.

Moroccan Lamb with Couscous

Osso Buco Express

Osso Buco Express

This Italian dish, usually made with thick veal shanks, is done in a flash with the help of a pressure cooker. We call for thinner—and less expensive—veal shoulder arm steaks (O bones). They may be labeled chops, but either way, be sure to look for the small round bone. Serve over rice if you like.

PREP: 5 MINUTES   COOK: 30 MINUTES   MAKES 6 MAIN-DISH SERVINGS

- 2 pounds bone-in veal shoulder arm steaks
- 1 tablespoon olive oil
- 1 bag (16 ounces) peeled baby carrots
- 8 ounces frozen small onions (half 16-ounce bag)
- 1 medium stalk celery, cut crosswise into 1/2-inch pieces
- 3 garlic cloves, minced
- 1/2 teaspoon salt
- 1/4 teaspoon freshly ground black pepper
- 1/4 teaspoon dried thyme
- 1 can (14 to 14 1/2 ounces) diced tomatoes
- 1/4 cup dry white wine
- 1/4 cup water
- 1/2 cup loosely packed fresh parsley, chopped
- 2 teaspoons grated fresh lemon peel

1. Pat veal dry with paper towels. In 6-quart pressure cooker, heat oil over high heat until hot. Add half the veal and cook until browned on both sides, using slotted spoon to transfer veal to bowl as it is browned. Repeat with remaining veal.

2. Add carrots, onions, celery, garlic, salt, pepper, and thyme and cook, stirring, 1 minute. Stir in tomatoes, wine, and water and heat to boiling over high heat.

3. Return veal to pressure cooker. Following manufacturer's directions, cover pressure cooker, bring up to pressure, and cook under pressure 15 minutes. Release pressure quickly, as manufacturer directs.

4. In cup, with fork, mix parsley and lemon peel; sprinkle over stew.

Each serving: About 220 calories, 29g protein, 13g carbohydrate, 6g total fat (1g saturated), 114mg cholesterol, 625mg sodium.

FISH & SHELLFISH

Corn and Shrimp Chowder, page 166

Shrimp Bisque

Bisque doesn't get any tastier than this. Serve it as an elegant first course or for lunch with a salad of greens and pears.

PREP: 30 MINUTES   COOK: 1 HOUR 10 MINUTES

MAKES ABOUT 10 CUPS OR 10 FIRST-COURSE SERVINGS

1 pound medium shrimp	2 tablespoons regular long-grain rice
3 tablespoons butter or margarine	1 1/4 teaspoons salt
2 cans (14 to 14 1/2 ounces each) reduced-sodium chicken broth, or 3 1/2 cups Chicken Broth (page 78)	1/8 to 1/4 teaspoon ground red pepper (cayenne)
1 cup dry white wine	1 bay leaf
1/2 cup water	1 can (14 to 14 1/2 ounces) diced tomatoes
2 medium carrots, chopped	1 cup half-and-half
2 medium stalks celery, chopped	2 tablespoons brandy or dry sherry
1 large onion (12 ounces), chopped	fresh chives for garnish

1. Shell and devein shrimp; reserve shells.

2. In nonreactive 5-quart Dutch oven, melt 1 tablespoon butter over medium heat. Add shrimp shells and cook, stirring often, 5 minutes.

3. Add broth, wine, and water and heat to boiling over high heat. Reduce heat to low; cover and simmer 15 minutes. Strain broth into 4-cup measuring cup or small bowl, pressing on shells with back of spoon to extract any remaining liquid. Discard shells.

4. In same Dutch oven, melt remaining 2 tablespoons butter over medium-high heat. Add shrimp and cook, stirring occasionally, until they turn opaque throughout, about 3 minutes. With slotted spoon, transfer shrimp to another small bowl.

5. Add carrots, celery, and onion to Dutch oven and cook, stirring occasionally, until lightly browned, 10 to 12 minutes.

6. Return broth mixture to Dutch oven. Add rice, salt, ground red pepper, and bay leaf and heat to boiling over high heat. Reduce heat to low; cover and simmer until rice is very tender, about 20 minutes. Add tomatoes with their juice and cook 10 minutes longer.

7. Remove Dutch oven from heat. Remove and discard bay leaf. Add shrimp.

8. Spoon one-fourth of shrimp mixture into blender; cover, with center part of lid removed to let steam escape, and puree until very smooth. Pour into large bowl. Repeat with each third of remaining mixture.

9. Return soup to Dutch oven. Add half-and-half and brandy; heat through over medium heat (do *not* boil or soup may curdle). Garnish with fresh chives.

Each serving: About 145 calories, 10g protein, 9g carbohydrate, 7g total fat (4g saturated), 74mg cholesterol, 739mg sodium.

Shrimp Savvy

- You can buy shrimp all year-round—about 95 percent of what's sold in the United States has been previously frozen.
- Depending on variety, shrimp shells can be light gray, brownish pink, or red, but when cooked, all will turn reddish.
- Select raw shrimp with firm-looking meat and shiny shells that feel full. Avoid black spots, which are a sign of aging. The heads are usually removed before shrimp are sold; if not, gently pull the head away from the body before shelling. Cooked, shelled shrimp should be plump with white flesh.
- When buying shrimp in their shells, always buy more than you need to account for the shelled weight. For example, 1 1/4 pounds shrimp yields 1 pound shelled and deveined.
- Shrimp can be shelled before or after cooking. Though shell-on shrimp can be more flavorful, it's often more convenient to shell before cooking.
- Deveining small and medium shrimp is optional. However, do remove the vein of large shrimp; it can contain grit.
- Although small shrimp are cheaper, they're harder to peel, and, pound for pound, may not be as good a value.
- Cook raw shrimp briefly, just until opaque throughout; heat cooked shrimp just until warmed through.
- Allow about 1/4 pound of shelled shrimp per serving.

Shrimp and Sausage Gumbo

Just like they make it on the bayou but easier, with frozen okra and canned broth. This Creole specialty is served with rice. Bake a pan of your favorite corn bread (from a mix or from scratch) to round out the meal.

PREP: 10 MINUTES   COOK: 40 MINUTES   MAKES 6 MAIN-DISH SERVINGS

1 cup regular long-grain rice
1 pound hot Italian-sausage links, casings pierced with a fork
3 tablespoons vegetable oil
1/4 cup all-purpose flour
2 medium stalks celery, cut into 1/4-inch pieces
1 medium green pepper, cut into 1/4-inch pieces
1 medium onion, cut into 1/4-inch pieces
1 can (14 to 14 1/2 ounces) chicken broth, or 1 3/4 cups Chicken Broth (page 74)

1 package (10 ounces) frozen whole okra
2 teaspoons hot pepper sauce
1/4 teaspoon dried thyme
1/4 teaspoon dried oregano
1 bay leaf
1/2 cup water
1 pound large shrimp, shelled and deveined, with tail part of shell left on
oregano sprigs (optional)

1. Prepare rice as label directs; keep warm.

2. Heat 5-quart Dutch oven or saucepot over medium-high heat until hot. Add sausages and cook, turning often, until very brown, about 10 minutes. With slotted spoon, transfer sausages to plate to cool slightly. Cut each sausage crosswise into thirds.

3. Discard all but 1 tablespoon drippings from Dutch oven. Add oil and heat over medium heat until hot. Stir in flour until blended and cook, stirring frequently, until flour is dark brown but not burned. Add celery, green pepper, and onion and cook, stirring occasionally, until tender, 8 to 10 minutes.

4. Return sausages to Dutch oven. Gradually stir in chicken broth, okra, hot pepper sauce, thyme, oregano, bay leaf, and water; heat to boiling. Reduce heat to low; cover and simmer 15 minutes. Add shrimp and cook, uncovered, until shrimp turn opaque throughout, about 2 minutes. Remove and discard bay leaf.

5. To serve, divide rice equally among 6 bowls and top with gumbo. Garnish with oregano sprigs, if you like.

Each serving:About 495 calories, 29g protein, 38g carbohydrate, 25g total fat (7g saturated), 144mg cholesterol, 820mg sodium.

Shrimp and Sausage Gumbo

Corn and Shrimp Chowder

This rich and tasty soup makes a delightfully satisfying meal on a cold night. We save time by boiling the potatoes while the bacon-and-onion mixture cooks. Buying cleaned shrimp is a time-saver, too.

PREP: 20 MINUTES   COOK: ABOUT 45 MINUTES

MAKES ABOUT 11 CUPS OR 10 FIRST-COURSE SERVINGS

1 pound red potatoes (about 3 medium), cut into 1/2-inch pieces	2 cups water
1 can (14 to 14 1/2 ounces) chicken broth, or 1 3/4 cups Chicken Broth (page 74)	2 packages (10 ounces each) frozen whole-kernel corn
1 teaspoon salt	2 slices bacon
1/4 teaspoon freshly ground black pepper	1 medium onion, chopped
	1 pound large shrimp, shelled and deveined
	1 cup half-and-half or light cream

1. In 4-quart saucepan, heat potatoes, broth, salt, pepper, and 1 cup water to boiling over high heat. Reduce heat to medium; cover and cook 10 minutes. Add 1 package frozen corn and cook just until potatoes are fork-tender, about 5 minutes longer.

2. Meanwhile, in 12-inch skillet, cook bacon over medium heat 5 minutes. Add onion and cook until onion is golden and tender, about 10 minutes longer. With slotted spoon, transfer bacon to paper towels to drain. When cool, break into pieces.

3. Add remaining 1 cup water and remaining package frozen corn to skillet with onion; heat to boiling over high heat. Add shrimp and cook until shrimp turn opaque, 4 to 5 minutes.

4. When potatoes are tender, transfer 2 cups potato mixture to blender with center part of lid removed to let steam escape, and puree mixture until smooth.

5. Return puree to saucepan. Add shrimp mixture and half-and-half; heat through (do *not* boil or soup may curdle). To serve, top each serving with bacon.

Each serving: About 370 calories, 23g protein, 39g carbohydrate, 15g total fat (6g saturated), 138mg cholesterol, 915mg sodium.

Clam and Bacon Chowder

This almost-homemade chowder is nearly as fast as take-out—but whole lot tastier.

PREP: 10 MINUTES   COOK: 20 MINUTES
MAKES ABOUT 7 1/2 CUPS OR 4 MAIN-DISH SERVINGS

2 slices bacon, cut into 1/2-inch
  pieces
2 large green onions
4 cups reduced-fat (2%) milk
1 bottle (8 ounces) clam juice
1 package (10 ounces) frozen
  cauliflower

1 package (4.9 to 5.25 ounces)
  dehydrated au gratin potatoes
1 can (10 ounces) whole baby clams,
  drained

1. In nonreactive 3-quart saucepan, cook bacon over medium heat until browned.

2. Meanwhile, thinly slice white and dark green parts of green onions. Reserve 2 tablespoons sliced dark green parts for garnish.

3. With slotted spoon, transfer bacon to paper towels to drain. Discard bacon drippings.

4. Add green onions (except reserved tops) to saucepan; cook, stirring, 30 seconds. Add milk, clam juice, frozen cauliflower, and au gratin cheese-sauce packet, stirring to blend. Cover and heat to boiling over high heat, stirring once.

5. Stir in potatoes. Reduce heat to medium-low and cook, covered, until potatoes are tender, about 8 minutes, stirring occasionally. Stir in clams and bacon; heat through. To serve, sprinkle with reserved green onion.

Each serving: About 355 calories, 26g protein, 43g carbohydrate, 9g total fat (4g saturated), 56mg cholesterol, 1,050mg sodium.

Oyster-Corn Chowder

Oyster-Corn Chowder

Oysters are the star of this delicious creamy chowder, chock-full of corn and potatoes. Perfect for Thanksgiving or any chilly day.

Prep: 20 minutes   Cook: about 40 minutes
Makes about 10 cups or 12 first-course servings

2 slices bacon, each cut crosswise
  in half
1 medium onion, finely chopped
1 pint shucked oysters (2 dozen),
  with their liquid
1 pound all-purpose potatoes (about
  3 medium), peeled and cut into
  1/4-inch pieces
2 bottles (8 ounces each) clam juice

1 cup half-and-half or light cream
1 can (15 to 16 ounces) whole-kernel
  corn, drained
2 cups whole milk
3/4 teaspoon salt
1/4 teaspoon freshly ground black
  pepper
1/4 cup snipped fresh chives plus
  chives for garnish

1. In nonreactive 4-quart saucepan, cook bacon over medium-low heat until browned. With slotted spoon, transfer bacon to paper towels to drain. When cool, crumble coarsely. Discard all but 1 teaspoon bacon drippings from saucepan.

2. Add onion to drippings in saucepan and cook over medium heat, stirring occasionally, until tender and golden, about 10 minutes.

3. Meanwhile, drain oysters, reserving oyster liquid. If necessary, add enough *water* to liquid to equal 2/3 cup.

4. Add potatoes, clam juice, and oyster liquid to onion in saucepan; heat to boiling over high heat. Reduce heat to medium-low; cover and simmer until potatoes are tender, about 10 minutes. Remove saucepan from heat.

5. With slotted spoon, transfer 1 cup solids to blender; cover, with center part of lid removed to let steam escape. Add half-and-half; cover and puree until smooth.

6. Return puree to saucepan. Stir in corn, milk, salt, and pepper; heat mixture just to boiling over medium-high heat. Add oysters and cook, stirring frequently, until oyster edges curl and centers are firm, 3 to 5 minutes. Stir in crumbled bacon and snipped chives. Garnish each serving with a few strands of fresh chives.

Each serving: About 125 calories, 5g protein, 16g carbohydrate, 5g total fat (3g saturated), 23mg cholesterol, 300mg sodium.

New England Cod Chowder

A classic, cozy winter warmer.

PREP: 50 MINUTES   COOK: 20 MINUTES

MAKES ABOUT 10 CUPS OF SOUP OR 5 MAIN-DISH SERVINGS

4 slices bacon
3 medium carrots, each cut lengthwise in half, then crosswise into slices
1 large fennel bulb (1 pound) or 3 stalks celery, cut into 1/4-inch pieces
1 medium onion, cut into 1/4-inch pieces

3 medium all-purpose potatoes (1 pound), peeled and cut into 1/2-inch pieces
3 bottles (8 ounces) clam juice
1 can (14 to 14 1/2 ounces) chicken broth, or 1 3/4 cups Chicken Broth (page 74)
1 bay leaf
1 cod fillet (1 pound), cut into 1 1/2-inch pieces
1 cup half-and-half or light cream

1. In nonreactive 5-quart Dutch oven or saucepot, cook bacon over medium heat until browned. With slotted spoon, transfer to paper towels to drain. When cool, crumble bacon.

2. Discard all but 2 tablespoons bacon drippings from Dutch oven. Add carrots, fennel, and onion and cook, stirring occasionally, until lightly browned, 6 to 8 minutes. Add potatoes, clam juice, broth, and bay leaf; heat to boiling. Reduce heat to low; cover and simmer until vegetables are tender, 10 to 15 minutes.

3. Add cod; cook, covered, until fish flakes easily when tested with a fork, 2 to 5 minutes. Carefully stir in half-and-half; heat through.

4. Remove and discard bay leaf. Serve soup with crumbled bacon.

Each serving: About 335 calories, 24g protein, 30g carbohydrate, 14g total fat (6g saturated), 72mg cholesterol, 780mg sodium.

Spring Fish Chowder

This delightful soup is filled with fresh vegetables and tender monkfish. The flavorful broth is accented with a touch of thyme, white wine, clam broth, and heavy cream.

PREP: 25 MINUTES   COOK: 25 MINUTES
MAKES ABOUT 8 CUPS OR 4 MAIN-DISH SERVINGS

1 tablespoon olive oil
3 medium carrots, cut crosswise into 1/2-inch pieces
2 stalks celery, cut into 1/4-inch-thick slices
1 bunch green onions, cut into 1/2-inch pieces
3 medium red potatoes (10 ounces), cut into 1-inch pieces
1 teaspoon salt
1/4 teaspoon coarsely ground black pepper
1/2 teaspoon dried thyme

1/2 cup dry white wine
1 bottle (8 ounces) clam juice
2 cups water
2 monkfish steaks (about 8 ounces each), dark membrane removed and cut into 1-inch pieces, or 1 pound scrod fillet, cut into 1-inch pieces
1 cup frozen peas
1/2 cup loosely packed fresh parsley, chopped
1/4 cup heavy or whipping cream

1. In nonstick 5-quart Dutch oven or saucepot, heat oil over medium-high heat until hot. Add carrots and celery; cook, stirring occasionally, until vegetables are lightly browned, about 6 minutes.
2. Stir in green onions, potatoes, salt, pepper, and thyme and cook 2 minutes longer. Add wine, clam juice, and water; heat to boiling. Reduce heat to low; cover and simmer 10 minutes.
3. Add fish and frozen peas; cover and simmer until vegetables are tender and fish is opaque throughout, about 5 minutes longer. Stir in parsley and cream; heat through (do *not* boil).

Each serving: About 295 calories, 20g protein, 29g carbohydrate, 11g total fat (4g saturated), 48mg cholesterol, 815mg sodium.

Peruvian Fisherman's Soup

A true treat for seafood lovers, this typically Peruvian mixture of shrimp and fish is spiced with chiles and brightened with lime.

PREP: 30 MINUTES   COOK: 25 MINUTES

MAKES ABOUT 11 CUPS OR 6 MAIN-DISH SERVINGS

1 tablespoon vegetable oil
1 medium onion, finely chopped
2 garlic cloves, minced
2 serrano or jalapeño chiles, seeded and minced
1 pound red potatoes, cut into 3/4-inch pieces
3 bottles (8 ounces each) clam juice
3/4 teaspoon salt

1/8 teaspoon dried thyme
2 cups water
1 lime
1 pound monkfish, dark membrane removed and cut into 1-inch pieces
1 pound medium shrimp, shelled and deveined, with tail part of shell left on, if you like
1/4 cup chopped fresh cilantro

1. In 4-quart saucepan, heat oil over medium heat until hot. Add onion and cook, stirring often, until tender, about 10 minutes. Stir in garlic and serranos and cook 30 seconds. Add potatoes, clam juice, salt, thyme, and water; heat to boiling over high heat. Reduce heat to low; simmer 10 minutes.

2. Cut lime in half; cut half into wedges and set aside. Add remaining lime half and monkfish to soup; cover and cook 5 minutes. Stir in shrimp and cook, just until shrimp turn opaque throughout, 3 to 5 minutes longer.

3. Remove lime half; squeeze juice into soup and discard rind. Sprinkle soup with cilantro; serve with lime wedges.

Each serving: About 215 calories, 26g protein, 16g carbohydrate, 5g total fat (1g saturated), 117mg cholesterol, 640mg sodium.

Peruvian Fisherman's Soup

Mussels in Saffron-Tomato Soup

Serve with crusty bread for dunking and an extra bowl for shells.

PREP: 20 MINUTES   COOK: 30 MINUTES

MAKES 4 MAIN-DISH SERVINGS

3 tablespoons olive oil
2 garlic cloves, crushed with side
  of chef's knife
1 small bay leaf
1/2 teaspoon loosely packed saffron
  threads
1/8 to 1/4 teaspoon crushed red
  pepper

1 can (14 to 14 1/2 ounces) diced
  tomatoes
1 bottle (8 ounces) clam juice
1/2 cup dry white wine
5 dozen medium mussels, scrubbed
  and debearded
chopped fresh parsley for garnish

1. In nonreactive 8-quart saucepot, heat oil over medium heat until hot. Add garlic and cook until golden. Add bay leaf, saffron threads, and crushed red pepper; cook, stirring, 1 minute.

2. Add tomatoes with their liquid, clam juice, and wine; heat to boiling over high heat. Reduce heat to low; cover and simmer 20 minutes.

3. Add mussels; heat to boiling over high heat. Reduce heat to medium; cover and cook until mussels open, about 4 to 5 minutes. Remove and discard bay leaf and any mussels that have not opened. Garnish with chopped parsley.

Each serving: About 220 calories, 15g protein, 10g carbohydrate, 13g total fat (2g saturated), 34mg cholesterol, 795mg sodium.

Cleaning Mussels

Scrub wild mussels well with a kitchen brush to remove grit. Cultivated varieties just need to be rinsed in cold water. If you purchase mussels with their "beard" or *byssus* (hairlike threads the mussel uses to attach itself to rocks or other surfaces) intact, remove it with a strong tug, no more than 1 or 2 hours before cooking.

Billi-Bi

There are many stories attributed to the origin of this soup—and almost as many versions of the recipe. Our blend of mussels in wine and cream is subtly seasoned with thyme and ground red pepper.

PREP: 20 MINUTES PLUS COOLING   COOK: 20 MINUTES
MAKES ABOUT 3 1/3 CUPS OR 4 FIRST-COURSE SERVINGS

2 pounds mussels, scrubbed and debearded	5 sprigs plus 1 tablespoon chopped fresh parsley
1 large onion (12 ounces), thinly sliced	pinch dried thyme
1 cup dry white wine	2 tablespoons all-purpose flour
1 cup water	1/2 cup heavy or whipping cream
	pinch ground red pepper (cayenne)
	salt (optional)

1. In nonreactive 5-quart Dutch oven, combine mussels, onion, wine, water, parsley sprigs, and thyme. Cover and heat to boiling over high heat. Reduce heat to medium; cook until mussels open, about 4 to 5 minutes, transferring mussels with slotted spoon to bowl as they open. Discard any mussels that have not opened.

2. When cool enough to handle, remove mussels from shells and discard shells. Strain mussel broth through sieve lined with paper towels into nonreactive 3-quart saucepan.

3. Heat mussel broth to boiling over high heat. In cup, with wire whisk, mix flour and cream until smooth; gradually whisk mixture into broth and heat to boiling, whisking. Add ground red pepper; reduce heat and simmer, whisking occasionally, 2 minutes.

4. Stir in mussels and heat through; do not overcook, or mussels will become tough. Taste and adjust for seasoning, adding salt, if necessary. Stir in chopped parsley.

Each serving without salt: About 236 calories, 10g protein, 12g carbohydrate, 13g total fat (7g saturated), 59mg cholesterol, 205mg sodium.

Mussel Soup

Mussel Soup

Easy and satisfying—serve with Italian bread to soak up every last drop.

PREP: 15 MINUTES   COOK: 20 MINUTES

MAKES ABOUT 10 CUPS OR 4 MAIN-DISH SERVINGS

1 tablespoon olive oil
1 large onion (12 ounces), sliced
2 garlic cloves, minced
1 can (28 ounces) plum tomatoes
   in puree
1 bottle (8 ounces) clam juice
1/2 cup dry white wine

1/4 teaspoon salt
1/8 teaspoon crushed red pepper
2 cups water
2 pounds small mussels, scrubbed
   and debearded
2 tablespoons chopped fresh parsley
2 green onions, chopped

1. In nonreactive 5-quart Dutch oven, heat oil over medium heat until hot. Add onion and cook until tender and lightly browned, about 10 minutes. Add garlic; cook 2 minutes longer.

2. Stir in tomatoes with their puree, clam juice, wine, salt, red pepper, and water and heat to boiling over high heat, stirring and breaking up tomatoes with back of spoon. Boil 3 minutes.

3. Add mussels; heat to boiling. Reduce heat to low; cover and simmer, stirring occasionally, until mussels open, about 4 to 5 minutes, transferring mussels to bowl as they open. Discard any mussels that have not opened.

4. Just before serving, stir in parsley and spoon broth over mussels. Garnish with green onions.

Each serving: About 160 calories, 11g protein, 16g carbohydrate, 6g total fat (1g saturated), 22mg cholesterol, 790mg sodium.

Bouillabaisse

Serve with thin slices of toasted French bread topped with generous dollops of aïoli, a garlic mayonnaise that originated in the Provence region of southern France.

PREP: 45 MINUTES   COOK: 1 HOUR

MAKES ABOUT 12 CUPS OR 6 MAIN-DISH SERVINGS

3 medium leeks (1 pound)
2 tablespoons olive oil
1 fennel bulb (about 1 pound), trimmed and thinly sliced
1 medium onion, coarsely chopped
2 garlic cloves, minced
1 cup dry white wine
2 bottles (8 ounces each) clam juice
1 can (14 to 14 1/2 ounces) whole tomatoes
3 strips (3" by 1" each) fresh orange peel
1 bay leaf
3/4 teaspoon salt
1/4 teaspoon dried thyme

1/8 teaspoon freshly ground black pepper
1/8 teaspoon ground red pepper (cayenne)
2 cups water
1 pound monkfish, dark membrane removed, cut into 1-inch pieces
1 dozen mussels, scrubbed and debearded
1 pound medium shrimp, shelled and deveined, with tail part of shell left on, if you like
1/4 cup loosely packed fresh parsley, chopped

1. Cut off roots and trim dark green tops from leeks; cut each leek lengthwise in half, then crosswise into thin slices. Rinse leeks in large bowl of cold water, swishing to remove sand. Transfer to colander to drain, leaving sand in bottom of bowl.

2. In nonreactive 5-quart Dutch oven, heat oil over medium-high heat until hot. Add leeks, fennel, onion, and garlic; cook, stirring occasionally, until vegetables are tender but not browned, 15 to 20 minutes.

3. Add wine and heat to boiling; boil 1 minute. Stir in clam juice, tomatoes with their juice, orange peel, bay leaf, salt, thyme, peppers, and water, breaking up tomatoes with side of spoon; heat to boiling. Reduce heat to low; cover and simmer 20 minutes to blend flavors. Remove and discard bay leaf.

4. Increase heat to medium-high. Stir in monkfish; cover and cook 3 minutes. Stir in mussels; cover and cook 1 minute. Stir in shrimp; cover and cook just until mussels open and fish and shrimp turn opaque throughout, 2 to 3 minutes. Discard any mussels that have not opened.
5. To serve, ladle Bouillabaisse into 6 large shallow soup bowls. Sprinkle with parsley.

Each serving: About 250 calories, 27g protein, 18g carbohydrate, 7g total fat (1g saturated), 118mg cholesterol, 770mg sodium.

Easy Aïoli

Aïoli (ay-OH-lee) is a very garlicky mayonnaise from Provence. Our recipe reduces the garlic's harshness by cooking it. Wonderful as a dip for vegetable or seafood, it is also the traditional condiment for Bouillabaisse.

In 2-quart saucepan combine 4 cups water and 1 teaspoon salt; heat to boiling. Add 14 cloves of unpeeled garlic (1 head) and boil until garlic has softened, about 20 minutes. Drain. When cool enough to handle, squeeze soft garlic from each clove into a small bowl. In blender, puree garlic, 1/2 cup mayonnaise, 2 teaspoons fresh lemon juice, 1/2 teaspoon Dijon mustard, 1/8 teaspoon salt, and 1/8 teaspoon ground red pepper (cayenne) until smooth. With blender running, through hole in lid, add 1/4 cup extra virgin olive oil in slow, steady stream until mixture is thickened and creamy. Transfer to small bowl; cover and refrigerate up to 4 hours. Makes about 1/4 cup.

California Cioppino

California Cioppino

This tomato-based stew has been popular in San Francisco since at least the 1930s and is served in many of the city's restaurants. It's believed to be a creation of the city's Italian immigrants and named after a Genovese fisherman's soup called *cioppin*.

PREP: 40 MINUTES   COOK: ABOUT 30 MINUTES

MAKES ABOUT 12 CUPS OR 6 MAIN-DISH SERVINGS

1 large lemon
2 tablespoons olive oil
2 medium red onions, each cut in half and thinly sliced
4 green onions, thinly sliced
3 garlic cloves, thinly sliced
1/2 cup dry white wine
1 medium yellow pepper, chopped
1 can (35 ounces) whole tomatoes in juice
1/2 teaspoon salt
1/8 teaspoon crushed red pepper
1/2 cup water

1 1/2 pounds striped bass or red snapper fillets, cut into 2-inch pieces
1 pound large shrimp, shelled and deveined, with tail part of shell left on if you like
1 pound mussels, scrubbed and debearded
1 cup loosely packed fresh parsley, chopped
1/4 cup loosely packed fresh basil, chopped

1. From lemon, remove 3 strips peel about 3" by 3/4" each; set aside.
2. In nonstick 5-quart Dutch oven, heat oil over medium heat until hot. Add lemon peel, red onions, green onions, and garlic and cook, stirring occasionally, 10 minutes. Add wine and yellow pepper; heat to boiling over medium-high heat. Reduce heat to medium-low, and simmer, stirring occasionally, 5 minutes.
3. Stir in tomatoes with their juice, salt, crushed red pepper, and water, breaking up tomatoes with side of spoon; heat to boiling over medium-high heat. Add fish, shrimp, mussels, and 1/4 cup parsley; heat to boiling. Reduce heat to medium-low and simmer, covered, 6 to 8 minutes, until fish and shrimp turn opaque throughout and mussels open.
4. Remove Dutch oven from heat; discard any mussels that have not opened. Stir in basil and remaining 3/4 cup parsley.

Each serving: About 305 calories, 39g protein, 16g carbohydrate, 9g total fat (2g saturated), 192mg cholesterol, 695mg sodium.

Seafood Stew

A festive, fresh seafood dish that cooks up quickly in ready-spiced tomato sauce.

PREP: 10 MINUTES   COOK: 20 MINUTES
MAKES 4 MAIN-DISH SERVINGS

1¹/₄ pounds all-purpose potatoes (about 4 medium), peeled and cut into ¹/₂-inch pieces

1 can (14¹/₂ ounces) chunky tomatoes with olive oil, garlic, and spices

1 can (14 to 14¹/₂ ounces) chicken broth, or 1³/₄ cups Chicken Broth (page 74)

¹/₃ cup dry white wine

16 large mussels, scrubbed and debearded

16 large shrimp, shelled and deveined, with tail part of shell left on

1 cod fillet (12 ounces), cut into 2-inch pieces

1 tablespoon chopped fresh parsley

1. In 2-quart saucepan, heat potatoes and enough *water* to cover to boiling over high heat. Reduce heat to low; cover and simmer until potatoes are tender, 5 to 8 minutes; drain.

2. Meanwhile, in 5-quart Dutch oven, heat tomatoes with their liquid, broth, and wine to boiling over high heat. Add mussels; reduce heat to medium. Cover and cook, transferring mussels to bowl as they open, 3 to 5 minutes. Discard any mussels that have not opened.

3. Add shrimp and cod to Dutch oven; cover and cook until shrimp and cod turn opaque throughout, 3 to 5 minutes. Add potatoes and mussels; heat through. To serve, sprinkle with parsley.

Each serving: About 305 calories, 35g protein, 28g carbohydrate, 5g total fat (0g saturated), 136mg cholesterol, 965mg sodium.

Seafood Stew

PASTA & BEAN

Macaroni, Cabbage, and Bean Soup, page 198

Pasta e Fagioli

A fast-lane version of our favorite Italian pasta and bean soup.

PREP: 5 MINUTES   COOK: 30 MINUTES
MAKES ABOUT 8 CUPS OR 4 MAIN-DISH SERVINGS

1 tablespoon olive oil
1 small onion, sliced
1 large stalk celery, sliced
1 can (14 to 14 1/2 ounces) chicken broth, or 1 3/4 cups Chicken Broth (page 74)
2 cups water
1 can (15 to 19 ounces) white kidney beans (cannellini), rinsed and drained

1 can (14 to 14 1/2 ounces) diced tomatoes
2 garlic cloves, crushed with garlic press
1 teaspoon sugar
1/4 teaspoon salt
1/4 teaspoon freshly ground black pepper
1/4 cup elbow macaroni, tubettini or ditalini pasta
1 package (10 ounces) frozen chopped spinach

1. In nonreactive 5- to 6-quart Dutch oven, heat oil over medium heat until hot. Add onion and celery and cook until vegetables are tender, about 10 minutes.

2. Meanwhile, in 2-quart saucepan, heat broth and water to boiling over high heat.

3. To Dutch oven, add beans, tomatoes, garlic, sugar, salt, and pepper; heat to boiling over high heat. Add broth mixture and pasta; heat to boiling. Reduce heat to medium and cook 5 minutes. Add frozen spinach; cook, stirring often to separate spinach, 3 to 4 minutes longer.

Each serving: About 220 calories, 10g protein, 33g carbohydrate, 5g total fat (1g saturated), 0mg cholesterol, 1,265mg sodium.

Tomato, Escarole, and Tortellini Soup

Perfect weeknight fare. You can use a bag of baby spinach instead of escarole, if you like.

PREP: 10 MINUTES   COOK: 10 MINUTES
MAKES ABOUT 7 1/2 CUPS OR 4 MAIN-DISH SERVINGS

1 package (8 ounces) frozen or 1
   package (9 ounces) fresh tortellini
   or mini ravioli
2 teaspoons olive oil
2 stalks celery, thinly sliced
1/2 medium head escarole, cut into
   bite-size pieces (about 5 cups)
1 can (14 to 14 1/2 ounces) diced
   tomatoes with sweet onions

1 can (14 to 14 1/2 ounces) chicken
   or vegetable broth, or 1 3/4 cups
   Chicken Broth (page 74) or
   Vegetable Broth (page 16)
1 cup water
1/4 cup freshly grated Romano
   cheese

1. Cook pasta as label directs.
2. Meanwhile, in 4-quart saucepan, heat oil over medium heat until hot. Add celery and cook, stirring occasionally, until tender-crisp, 5 minutes. Stir in escarole, tomatoes, broth, and water. Cover and heat to boiling over high heat. Remove saucepan from heat.
3. Drain tortellini; gently stir into broth mixture. Divide soup equally among 4 large bowls; sprinkle each serving with 1 tablespoon grated Romano.

Each serving: About 200 calories, 10g protein, 25g carbohydrate, 7g total fat (3g saturated), 14mg cholesterol, 1,185mg sodium.

Pasta e Piselli

One fast soup; just 10 minutes to prepare, 15 minutes to cook. Cousin to the Italian favorite Pasta e Fagioli (see page 186), this is made with peas instead. Dust with freshly grated Parmesan or Pecorino Romano for an irresistible touch.

PREP: 10 MINUTES   COOK: 15 MINUTES

MAKES ABOUT 10 CUPS OR 5 MAIN-DISH SERVINGS

2 cups mixed pasta, such as penne, bow tie, or elbow macaroni (about 8 ounces)
2 tablespoons olive oil
3 garlic cloves, crushed with side of chef's knife
2 cans (14 to 14 1/2 ounces each) chicken broth or 3 1/2 cups Chicken Broth (page 74)

1 can (14 to 14 1/2 ounces) diced tomatoes
1/4 cup packed fresh basil, coarsely chopped
1/2 cup water
1 package (10 ounces) frozen peas, thawed
freshly grated Parmesan or Pecorino Romano cheese

1. Cook pasta as label directs.
2. Meanwhile, in nonreactive 4-quart saucepan or saucepot, heat oil over medium heat until hot. Add garlic; cook until golden, about 5 minutes.
3. Remove saucepan from heat, then carefully add broth, tomatoes with their juice, basil, and water. Return to heat; heat to boiling. Reduce heat to low; cover and simmer 5 minutes. Remove and discard garlic.
4. Stir in peas and pasta; heat through. Serve with Parmesan.

Each serving: About 400 calories, 11g protein, 46g carbohydrate, 7g total fat (1g saturated), 8mg cholesterol, 705mg sodium.

Pasta e Piselli

Asian-Style Noodle Soup

Our homemade version of the take-out classic.

Prep: 15 minutes   Cook: about 20 minutes
Makes about 13 cups or 6 main-dish servings

4 ounces dried flat rice noodles
(about 1/4 inch wide)
2 teaspoons vegetable oil
1 tablespoon minced, peeled fresh
ginger
1 large garlic clove, crushed with
garlic press
2 teaspoons ground coriander
2 pieces (about 3 inches long each)
dried or fresh lemongrass (optional)
3 green onions, thinly sliced

2 cans (14 to 14 1/2 ounces each)
chicken broth, or 3 1/2 cups
Chicken Broth (page 74)
1/4 cup Asian fish sauce
4 cups water
1 pound skinless, boneless chicken
thighs, cut into 1/2-inch-thick slices
1 small head napa (Chinese) cabbage
(about 1 pound), cored and cut
crosswise into 1/2-inch-wide strips
1/2 cup loosely packed fresh mint

1. In large bowl, pour enough *hot water* over rice noodles to cover; let soak until softened, about 10 minutes.

2. Meanwhile, in 4-quart saucepan, heat oil over medium heat until hot. Add ginger and garlic and cook 30 seconds. Stir in coriander and lemongrass, if using, and cook, stirring, 30 seconds. Add green onions and cook 2 minutes.

3. Stir in broth, fish sauce, and water; cover and heat to boiling over high heat.

4. Drain noodles. Stir noodles, chicken, cabbage, and mint into broth mixture; cook until chicken just loses its pink color throughout, about 4 minutes. Remove and discard lemongrass.

Each serving: About 210 calories, 20g protein, 21g carbohydrate, 15g total fat (1g saturated), 63mg cholesterol, 1,120mg sodium.

Spring Soup with Noodles, Ham, and Asparagus

Using ramen noodle-soup mix and sliced ham from the deli keeps preparation to a bare minimum—perfect for an impromptu family meal.

Prep: 10 minutes   Cook: 15 minutes

Makes about 9 cups or 4 main-dish servings

7 cups water
2 teaspoons vegetable oil
1 large red pepper, thinly sliced
1 pound asparagus, trimmed and cut diagonally into 2-inch pieces

4 ounces sliced deli baked ham, cut into 1/2-inch-wide strips
2 packages (3 ounces each) chicken-flavored ramen noodle-soup mix
2 teaspoons Asian sesame oil

1. In 4-quart saucepan, heat water to boiling over high heat.
2. Meanwhile, in nonstick 12-inch skillet, heat oil over medium-high heat until hot. Add red pepper and asparagus and cook until vegetables are tender-crisp, about 7 minutes. Stir in ham and cook until ham is heated through, about 1 minute.
3. Stir ramen noodles with their seasoning packets into boiling water; boil until noodles are tender, about 2 minutes. Remove from heat; stir in ham mixture and sesame oil.

Each serving: About 300 calories, 12g protein, 31g carbohydrate, 15g total fat (5g saturated), 15mg cholesterol, 1,205mg sodium.

Vegetable Soup with Bow Ties and Dill

Vegetable Soup with Bow Ties and Dill

Chicken broth brimming with sautéed vegetables and tiny pasta is seasoned with a hint of lemon and lots of fresh dill—a perfect beginning to a light feast!

PREP: 25 MINUTES   COOK: ABOUT 30 MINUTES

MAKES ABOUT 9 CUPS OR 8 FIRST-COURSE SERVINGS

1 lemon
1 tablespoon olive oil
1 large shallot, finely chopped
4 medium carrots, cut lengthwise
  into quarters, then thinly sliced
  crosswise
2 medium stalks celery, thinly sliced
About 3 1/2 cans (14 to 14 1/2 ounces
  each) fat-free chicken broth or 6
  cups Chicken Broth (page 74)

1 cup water
1 package (10 ounces) frozen peas
3/4 cup small bow-tie pasta, cooked
  as label directs
3 tablespoons chopped dill
1/8 teaspoon freshly ground black
  pepper

1. With vegetable peeler or small knife, remove 3" by 1" strip peel from lemon; squeeze 1 tablespoon juice.

2. In nonstick 5- to 6-quart saucepot, heat oil over medium-high heat until hot. Add shallot and cook, stirring frequently, until golden, about 2 minutes. Add carrots and celery and cook, stirring occasionally, until tender-crisp, 5 minutes.

3. Add broth, lemon peel, and water to saucepot; heat to boiling over medium-high heat. Reduce heat to low; cover and simmer until vegetables are tender, about 10 minutes.

4. Remove cover; stir in frozen peas and cook 1 minute longer. Stir in cooked pasta, dill, pepper, and lemon juice; heat through.

Each serving: About 120 calories, 5g protein, 17g carbohydrate, 2g total fat (1g saturated), 0mg cholesterol, 770mg sodium.

Thai Coconut Soup with Bean-Thread Noodles

This exotic-tasting soup is easy to whip up for a light supper. Our version uses chicken—or try it with tofu.

PREP: 25 MINUTES   COOK: 20 MINUTES

MAKES ABOUT 10 1/2 CUPS OR 4 MAIN-DISH SERVINGS

4 ounces bean-thread noodles (also called saifun, cellophane, or glass noodles)

1 can (14 ounces) light unsweetened coconut milk (not cream of coconut), well stirred

2 garlic cloves, crushed with garlic press

1 tablespoon minced, peeled fresh ginger

1/2 teaspoon ground coriander

1/2 teaspoon ground cumin

1/4 teaspoon ground red pepper (cayenne)

3 small skinless, boneless chicken-breast halves (12 ounces), thinly sliced, or 1 package (1 pound) firm tofu, rinsed, drained, and cut into 1-inch cubes

2 cans (14 to 14 1/2 ounces each) low-sodium chicken broth or vegetable broth, or 3 1/2 cups Chicken Broth (page 74) or Vegetable Broth (page 16)

2 green onions, thinly sliced

2 small carrots, cut into 2" by 1/4" matchstick strips

1/2 medium red pepper, cut into 2" by 1/4" matchstick strips

1 tablespoon Asian fish sauce (*nuoc nam*, see note)

1 cup water

2 tablespoons fresh lime juice

1 cup loosely packed fresh cilantro, chopped

1. In large saucepot, heat *3 quarts water* to boiling over high heat; remove saucepot from heat. Place noodles in water; soak just until transparent (do not oversoak), 10 to 15 minutes.

2. Meanwhile, in 5-quart Dutch oven, heat 1/2 cup coconut milk to boiling over medium heat. Add garlic, ginger, coriander, cumin, and ground red pepper and cook, stirring, 1 minute. Increase heat to medium-high; add chicken and cook, stirring constantly, just until chicken loses its pink color throughout. (If using tofu, add with remaining coconut milk in Step 3.)

3. Drain noodles. Rinse with cold running water and drain again. With kitchen shears, cut noodles into shorter lengths.

4. To mixture in Dutch oven, add broth, green onions, carrots, red pepper, fish sauce, water, remaining coconut milk, and tofu, if using, and the cooked noodles; heat just to simmering over medium-high heat, stirring occasionally. Stir in lime juice and cilantro just before serving.

Each serving: About 340 calories, 25g protein, 34g carbohydrate, 11g total fat (6g saturated), 53mg cholesterol, 525mg sodium.

Note: Asian fish sauce is available in specialty sections of some supermarkets and in Asian groceries.

Using Their Noodles:
The Joy of Asian Soups

Noodle soup started out as a peasant food in China; workers visited noodle shops for filling, inexpensive meals. Today, noodle houses are big business in many parts of Asia. Each type of soup traditionally uses one type of noodle, but any of the noodles listed here can be substituted for one another. These are available in Asian markets, specialty stores, and some supermarkets. (All noodles are dried unless otherwise noted.)

Bean Thread (or Cellophane) Noodles: made from mung bean starch; they become translucent when cooked.

Instant (or Ramen) Noodles: made from wheat flour; precooked (usually fried); need just a quick boil.

Rice Noodles: made from rice flour; also called rice sticks or rice vermicelli; must soak 20 to 60 minutes before using. (Fresh rice noodles, *sha he fen,* are available in flat sheets that can be cut to desired size.)

Te'uchi: fresh; made from wheat flour; similar to *lo mein* (below), but hand-made, so more expensive.

Wheat Flour Noodles: usually fresh, sometimes dried; called *lo mein* in Chinese; *somen* or *soba* (buckwheat) in Japanese. Somen are sometimes colored green (with green-tea powder), yellow (with egg), or pink (with Japanese red basil oil).

Vietnamese Noodle Soup

This Asian-style broth is chock-full of delicate rice noodles, fresh snow peas, shiitake mushrooms, and pungent herbs. Called *pho* (pronounced FUH) in Vietnamese, it is named for the wide rice noodles it contains.

PREP: 20 MINUTES   COOK: 25 MINUTES

MAKES ABOUT 9 CUPS OR 4 MAIN-DISH SERVINGS

1 large lime
4 ounces dried flat rice noodles
  (about 1/4 inch wide)
2 cans (14 to 14 1/2 ounces each)
  chicken broth or vegetable broth or
  3 1/2 cups Chicken Broth (page 74)
  or Vegetable Broth (page 16)
1 small bunch fresh basil
2 garlic cloves, crushed with side of
  chef's knife

1 piece (2 inches) peeled, fresh
  ginger, thinly sliced
2 cups water
1/4 pound shiitake mushrooms, stems
  removed and caps thinly sliced
4 ounces snow peas, strings removed
  and each pod cut diagonally in half
1 tablespoon soy sauce
1 cup loosely packed fresh cilantro,
  chopped

1. From lime, with vegetable peeler, remove peel and reserve; squeeze 1 tablespoon juice.

2. In large bowl, pour enough *boiling water* over rice noodles to cover; let soak until softened, 7 to 10 minutes.

3. Meanwhile, in 3-quart saucepan, heat broth, basil, garlic, ginger, lime peel, and water to boiling over high heat. Reduce heat to low; cover and simmer 10 minutes. Strain broth through sieve set over medium bowl, pressing with back of spoon to extract any remaining liquid; discard solids. Return broth to saucepan.

4. Drain noodles; rinse under cold running water and drain again. Stir mushrooms, snow peas, soy sauce, and noodles into broth mixture; heat to boiling over high heat. Reduce heat to low; cover and simmer 3 minutes. Stir in cilantro and lime juice just before serving.

Each serving: About 155 calories, 5g protein, 30g carbohydrate, 2g total fat (1g saturated), 0mg cholesterol, 1,120mg sodium.

Vietnamese Noodle Soup

Macaroni, Cabbage, and Bean Soup

A light yet chunky vegetable soup that's ready in less than half an hour.

PREP: 5 MINUTES   COOK: 15 MINUTES
MAKES 12 CUPS OR 6 MAIN-DISH SERVINGS

1 1/2 cups elbow macaroni or mini penne pasta
salt
1 tablespoon olive oil
1 medium onion, cut in half and thinly sliced
1/2 small head savoy cabbage (about 1 pound), thinly sliced
2 garlic cloves, crushed with garlic press

1/4 teaspoon ground black pepper
3 cans (14 to 14 1/2 ounces each) chicken broth, or 5 1/4 cups Chicken Broth (page 74)
1 1/2 cups water
2 cans (15 to 19 ounces each) white kidney beans (cannellini), rinsed and drained
freshly grated Parmesan or Pecorino Romano cheese (optional)

1. Cook macaroni as label directs.

2. Meanwhile, in 5- to 6-quart saucepot, heat oil over medium-high heat until hot. Add onion, cabbage, garlic, and pepper; cook, stirring often, until cabbage begins to wilt, 6 to 8 minutes. Stir in broth, beans, and water; heat to boiling.

3. Meanwhile, drain macaroni. Stir macaroni into cabbage mixture; heat through. Serve with Parmesan, if you like.

Each serving: About 310 calories, 14g protein, 52g carbohydrate, 5g total fat (1g saturated), 0mg cholesterol, 1,170mg sodium.

Hearty Minestrone

Your guests will welcome a steaming bowl of this vegetable-bean soup on a cold winter night. It tastes even better reheated, so it's a good choice to prepare in advance.

PREP: 45 MINUTES   COOK: 30 MINUTES
MAKES ABOUT 20 CUPS OR 10 MAIN-DISH SERVINGS

2 slices bacon, chopped
2 medium carrots, peeled and cut into 1/4-inch pieces
1 medium onion, cut into 1/4-inch pieces
1 large stalk celery, cut into 1/4-inch pieces
2 garlic cloves, minced
3 medium all-purpose potatoes (about 1 pound), peeled and cut into 1/4-inch pieces
1 can (14 to 14 1/2 ounces) chicken broth or 1 3/4 cups Chicken Broth (page 74)
1 1/4 teaspoons salt
1/4 teaspoon coarsely ground black pepper

1/4 teaspoon dried thyme
6 cups water
1 can (15 1/ to 19 ounces) white kidney beans (cannellini), rinsed and drained
1/2 pound green beans, trimmed and cut into 1-inch pieces
1/3 cup small pasta, such as cavatelli, tubettini, or ditalini
1 pound Swiss chard, tough stems trimmed and leaves chopped
1/2 pound spinach, tough stems trimmed
1/2 teaspoon freshly grated lemon peel
grated Parmesan or Pecorino Romano cheese (optional)

1. In 6-quart saucepot, cook bacon over medium heat until browned. With slotted spoon, transfer bacon to paper towels to drain; set aside.

2. To drippings in saucepot, add carrots, onion, and celery and cook, stirring occasionally, until vegetables are browned, about 15 minutes. Add garlic and cook 30 seconds longer.

3. Add potatoes, broth, salt, pepper, thyme, and water; heat to boiling over high heat. Reduce heat to low; cover and simmer 10 minutes.

4. Add white beans, green beans, and pasta; cook 7 minutes longer. Stir in Swiss chard, spinach, and lemon peel; cook until greens are wilted and tender, about 5 minutes longer. Stir in bacon. Serve with grated Parmesan, if you like.

Each serving: About 370 calories, 5g protein, 17g carbohydrate, 2g total fat (1g saturated), 2mg cholesterol, 440mg sodium.

Minestrone with Pesto

Minestrone with Pesto

The classic rich, thick Italian soup, made with dried beans, bacon, potatoes, and—for a tasty new twist—easy homemade (or prepared) pesto.

PREP: 30 MINUTES PLUS SOAKING BEANS   COOK: 1 HOUR
MAKES ABOUT 13 CUPS OR 6 MAIN-DISH SERVINGS

8 ounces dry Great Northern beans
   (about 1¹/₃ cups), rinsed and
   picked through
2 tablespoons olive oil
3 medium carrots, sliced
2 stalks celery, sliced
1 large onion (12 ounces), cut into
   ¹/₄-inch pieces
2 ounces pancetta or bacon, cut into
   ¹/₄-inch pieces
1 pound all-purpose potatoes, peeled
   and cut into ¹/₂-inch cubes
2 medium zucchini (8 ounces each),
   ends trimmed and each cut
   lengthwise into quarters, then
   crosswise into ¹/₄-inch-thick pieces

¹/₂ medium head savoy cabbage
   (1 pound), thinly sliced to equal
   4 cups
1 large garlic clove, crushed with
   garlic press
2 cans (14 to 14¹/₂ ounces each)
   chicken broth or 3¹/₂ cups Chicken
   Broth (page 74)
1 can (14 to 14¹/₂ ounces) diced
   tomatoes
1 cup water
¹/₂ teaspoon salt
Pesto (page 202) or ¹/₂ cup store-
   bought pesto

1. In large bowl, place beans with enough *water to cover by 2 inches*. Soak overnight. (Or, in 4-quart saucepan, heat beans and *6 cups water* to boiling over high heat; cook 2 minutes. Remove from heat; cover and let stand 1 hour.) Drain and rinse beans.

2. In 4-quart saucepan, heat beans and enough *water to cover by 2 inches* to boiling over high heat. Reduce heat to low; cover and simmer, stirring occasionally, until beans are tender, 40 minutes to 1 hour. Drain beans.

3. While beans are cooking, in 5-quart Dutch oven, heat oil over medium-high heat until hot. Add carrots, celery, onion, and pancetta; cook, stirring occasionally, until onions begin to brown, about 10 minutes. Add potatoes, zucchini, cabbage, and garlic; cook, stirring constantly, until cabbage has wilted.

(continued on page 202)

4. Add broth, tomatoes with their juice, and water; heat to boiling over high heat. Reduce heat to low; cover and simmer until vegetables are tender, about 30 minutes.

5. Meanwhile, prepare Pesto.

6. Spoon 1/2 cup beans and 1 cup soup mixture into blender or food processor with knife blade attached; puree until smooth. Stir salt, bean puree, and remaining beans into soup; heat to boiling. Reduce heat to low; cover and simmer 10 minutes. Garnish with dollops of Pesto.

Pesto

Spoon *2/3 cup packed fresh basil, 1/4 cup grated Parmesan cheese, 1/4 cup olive oil, 1 tablespoon water, and 1/4 teaspoon salt* into blender and puree until smooth. Makes about 1/2 cup.

Each serving with pesto: About 425 calories, 16g protein, 45g carbohydrate, 22g total fat (5g saturated), 17mg cholesterol, 955mg sodium.

Do-ahead tip: Pesto is great in soup and as a sauce on pasta. Make large batches ahead of time and freeze in ice cube trays to have a quick homemade sauce on hand. Just defrost and serve!

Escarole and Bean Soup

This soup is perfect when you need to get a homey dinner on the table in a hurry. Our secret ingredient is pesto, which adds delectable flavor. Serve soup with freshly grated Parmesan cheese or additional pesto.

PREP: 15 MINUTES   COOK: 15 MINUTES

MAKES ABOUT 9 CUPS OR 4 MAIN-DISH SERVINGS

1/2 cup small elbow macaroni

1 can (15 to 19 ounces) white kidney beans (cannellini), rinsed and drained

2 cans (14 to 14 1/2 ounces each) chicken broth or 3 1/2 cups Chicken Broth (page 74)

3 cups water

1 large head escarole (10 ounces), coarsely chopped

2 tablespoons prepared pesto or Pesto (opposite)

1. Cook pasta as label directs, omitting salt.
2. Meanwhile, in small bowl, with fork, mash 1/2 cup beans until almost smooth; set aside.
3. In 4-quart saucepan, heat broth and water to boiling over high heat.
4. Drain pasta. Add pasta, mashed and whole beans, and escarole to broth mixture; heat to boiling. Reduce heat to low; simmer, stirring occasionally, until escarole is tender, about 5 minutes. Stir in pesto.

Each serving: About 225 calories, 13g protein, 31g carbohydrate, 6g total fat (1g saturated), 2mg cholesterol, 960mg sodium.

Tuscan Vegetable-Bean Soup

Healthy and hearty—dust with freshly grated Parmesan cheese.

PREP: 45 MINUTES PLUS OVERNIGHT TO SOAK BEANS

COOK: ABOUT 1 HOUR 30 MINUTES

MAKES ABOUT 14 CUPS OR 6 MAIN-DISH SERVINGS

8 ounces dry Great Northern beans
(1 1/3 cups), rinsed and picked
through
5 medium carrots, peeled
1 jumbo onion (1 pound)
1 bay leaf
6 cups water
3 tablespoons olive oil
4 ounces pancetta or cooked ham,
chopped
3 large stalks celery, coarsely
chopped
1 small fennel bulb (1 pound),
trimmed and coarsely chopped

2 garlic cloves, finely chopped
2 cans (14 to 14 1/2 ounces each)
chicken broth, or 3 1/2 cups
Chicken Broth (page 74)
1 pound all-purpose potatoes
(3 medium), peeled and cut into
1/2-inch pieces
1 medium head escarole
(12 ounces), cut crosswise into
1/4-inch-thick strips
1/2 teaspoon salt
grated Parmesan cheese (optional)

1. Rinse beans with cold running water and discards any stones or shriveled beans. In large bowl, place beans with enough *water* to cover by 2 inches. Soak overnight. (Or, in 4-quart saucepan, heat beans and *8 cups water* to boiling over high heat; cook 2 minutes. Remove from heat; cover and let stand 1 hour.) Drain and rinse beans.

2. Cut 1 carrot crosswise in half. Coarsely chop remaining carrots; set aside. Cut onion into 4 wedges. Leave 1 wedge whole; coarsely chop remaining wedges.

3. In 4-quart saucepan, combine beans, carrot halves, onion wedge, bay leaf, and water; heat to boiling over high heat. Reduce heat to low; cover and simmer, stirring occasionally, until beans are tender, 40 minutes to 1 hour. Drain beans and vegetables, reserving 3 cups cooking liquid. Discard carrot halves and onion wedge.

4. Meanwhile, in 5-quart saucepot or Dutch oven, heat oil over medium-high heat until hot. Add pancetta, celery, fennel, chopped

carrots, and coarsely chopped onion; cook, stirring occasionally, until vegetables begin to brown, about 15 minutes. Add garlic; cook, stirring, 1 minute.

5. Stir in broth, cooked beans, reserved 3 cups cooking liquid, potatoes, and escarole; heat to boiling over high heat. Reduce heat to low; cover and simmer until all vegetables are very tender, 15 to 20 minutes. Discard bay leaf. Stir in salt. Serve with Parmesan, if you like.

Each serving: About 335 calories, 17g protein, 48g carbohydrate, 10g total fat (2g saturated), 18mg cholesterol, 935mg sodium.

Do Dry Beans Need to be Soaked?

It's common knowledge that soaking dry beans for hours before using shortens cooking time and improves texture, appearance, and even digestibility. But now some chefs are claiming soaking time can be reduced—even skipped. We tested the old-fashioned method against two shortcuts in the *Good Housekeeping* kitchens, using three batches of black beans and three of Great Northern beans, which were then cooked until tender. The results:

The Winner Is... Overnight Soaking. Grandma was right. For the best texture (not too hard or mushy) and appearance (beans held their shape, with practically no split skins), letting beans sit in a bowl of cool tap water until morning really works. Cooking time ranged from 1 hour and 10 minutes to 1 hour and 20 minutes.

Second Place: No Soaking. This method yielded the second most tender and shapely beans, though it required the longest cooking time (1 hour and 35 minutes). But if beans pose digestive problems for you, it's probably better to soak them and discard the water, which helps remove the complex sugars that can cause bloating and gas.

Third Place: Quick Soaking. Bringing the beans to a boil for 2 minutes and then allowing them to soak for an hour in the same water before cooking yielded the most broken beans but definitely the fastest cooking time (1 hour). If you're making a bean soup or chili, where perfect-looking beans don't matter, this method is fine, but we don't recommend it for a bean salad.

Note: Whichever option you choose, remember that cooking time will vary depending on the age/dryness of the beans.

Creamy Italian White-Bean Soup

A perfect marriage of canned beans and fresh spinach, with a squeeze of fresh lemon juice for flavor.

PREP: 15 MINUTES   COOK: 40 MINUTES

MAKES ABOUT 6 CUPS OR 4 MAIN-DISH SERVINGS

1 tablespoon vegetable oil
1 medium onion, finely chopped
1 medium stalk celery, finely chopped
1 garlic clove, minced
2 cans (15 to 19 ounces each) white kidney beans (cannellini), rinsed and drained
1 can (14 to 14 1/2 ounces) chicken broth, or 1 3/4 cups Chicken Broth (page 74)

1/4 teaspoon coarsely ground black pepper
1/8 teaspoon dried thyme
1 bunch (10 to 12 ounces) spinach
1 tablespoon fresh lemon juice
freshly grated Parmesan or Pecorino Romano cheese (optional)

1. In 3-quart saucepan, heat oil over medium heat until hot. Add onion and celery and cook, stirring occasionally, until tender, 5 to 8 minutes. Add garlic; cook, stirring, 30 seconds. Add beans, broth, pepper, thyme, and water; heat to boiling over high heat. Reduce heat to low; simmer, uncovered, 15 minutes.

2. Meanwhile, remove tough stems from spinach and discard; thinly slice leaves.

3. With slotted spoon, remove 2 cups bean-and-vegetable mixture from soup; set aside. Spoon half of remaining mixture into blender, cover, with center part of lid removed to let steam escape, and puree until smooth. Pour puree into large bowl. Repeat with remaining soup.

4. Return soup to saucepan. Stir in reserved beans and vegetables; heat to boiling over high heat, stirring occasionally. Stir in spinach and cook until wilted, about 1 minute. Stir in lemon juice and remove from heat. Serve with Parmesan, if you like.

Each serving without Parmesan: About 295 calories, 18g protein, 46g carbohydrate, 5g total fat (1g saturated), 0mg cholesterol, 945mg sodium.

Creamy Italian White-Bean Soup

Senate Bean Soup

Stories abound on the origins of the recipe for this famous white-bean soup, but the mandate for serving it in the Senate dining rooms dates to the first decade of the twentieth century, when the chairman of the Senate Committee on Rules and Administration enjoyed the soup so much that he decreed it should be served on a daily basis.

PREP: 20 MINUTES PLUS SOAKING BEANS   COOK: ABOUT 1 HOUR 15 MINUTES
MAKES ABOUT 8 1/4 CUPS OR 8 FIRST-COURSE SERVINGS

1 pound dry Great Northern beans, rinsed and picked through
2 tablespoons olive oil
1 large smoked ham hock
1 medium onion, chopped
1 medium carrot, chopped
1 medium stalk celery, chopped
2 garlic cloves, finely chopped
1 carton (32 ounces) chicken or vegetable broth or 4 cups Chicken Broth (page 74) or Vegetable Broth (page 16)

6 ounces deli ham in 1 piece, cut into 1/2-inch pieces (about 1 cup)
1 teaspoon salt
1/4 teaspoon freshly ground black pepper
2 medium tomatoes, coarsely chopped
1/4 cup chopped fresh parsley
2 tablespoons fresh lemon juice

1. In large bowl, place beans and enough *water* to cover by 2 inches. Cover and let stand at room temperature overnight. Drain and rinse beans.

2. In 4-quart saucepan, heat oil over medium heat until hot. Add ham hock and onion and cook, stirring occasionally, until onion is tender and lightly browned, 8 to 10 minutes. Add carrot, celery, and garlic, and cook, stirring occasionally, 5 minutes longer.

3. Add broth and beans to saucepan; heat to boiling over high heat. Reduce heat to low; cover and simmer until beans are tender, about 1 hour.

4. Remove ham hock; cool slightly. Dice meat and add to soup. Cover and cook 15 minutes to blend flavors.

5. To serve, ladle soup into 8 bowls; top with tomatoes, parsley, and lemon juice.

Each serving: About 295 calories, 18g protein, 42g carbohydrate, 7g total fat (2g saturated), 11mg cholesterol, 1,085mg sodium.

Source: U.S. Senate

Cranberry-Bean Soup

A Chilean-style soup made with butternut squash, tomatoes, fresh basil, and jalapeño. Cranberry beans have large, knobby beige pods speckled with red; the beans inside are cream-colored with red streaks and have a nutlike taste.

PREP: 40 MINUTES   COOK: 45 MINUTES

MAKES ABOUT 9 CUPS OR 4 MAIN-DISH SERVINGS

4 teaspoons olive oil
1 medium butternut squash (2 pounds), peeled and cut into 3/4-inch pieces
1 medium onion, chopped
2 garlic cloves, minced
1 jalapeño chile, seeded and minced
1 teaspoon ground cumin
1 can (14 to 14 1/2 ounces) chicken broth or 1 3/4 cups Chicken Broth (page 74)

2 medium tomatoes, diced
1 1/2 pounds fresh cranberry beans, shelled (about 2 cups)
1 teaspoon salt
1 teaspoon sugar
1 1/2 cups loosely packed fresh basil, chopped
2 1/2 cups water
2 cups corn kernels cut from cobs (about 4 medium ears)

1. In 5-quart Dutch oven, heat 2 teaspoons oil over medium heat until hot. Add squash and onion and cook, stirring occasionally, until golden, about 10 minutes. Transfer squash mixture to medium bowl.
2. In same Dutch oven, heat remaining 2 teaspoons oil over medium heat; add garlic, pepper, and cumin and cook, stirring, 1 minute. Stir in broth, tomatoes, beans, salt, sugar, squash mixture, 1/4 cup chopped basil, and water; heat to boiling over high heat. Reduce heat to low; cover and simmer, stirring occasionally, until beans are tender, about 30 minutes.
3. Stir in corn; heat to boiling over high heat. Reduce heat to low; cover and simmer 5 minutes longer. Stir in remaining 1 1/4 cups chopped basil.

Each serving: About 360 calories, 16g protein, 66g carbohydrate, 7g total fat (1g saturated), 0mg cholesterol, 890mg sodium.

Caribbean Black-Bean Soup

Caribbean Black-Bean Soup

This take on black-bean soup is made with sweet potatoes and fresh cilantro for great flavor.

PREP: 45 MINUTES PLUS SOAKING BEANS COOK: 2 HOURS 30 MINUTES

MAKES ABOUT 13 CUPS OR 6 MAIN-DISH SERVINGS

1 package (16 ounces) dry black beans, rinsed and picked through
2 tablespoons vegetable oil
2 medium red onions, chopped
4 jalapeño chiles, seeded and minced
2 tablespoons minced, peeled fresh ginger
4 garlic cloves, minced
1/2 teaspoon ground allspice
1/2 teaspoon dried thyme

8 cups water
2 medium sweet potatoes (about 1 1/2 pounds), peeled and cut into 3/4-inch pieces
1 tablespoon dark brown sugar
2 teaspoons salt
1 bunch green onions, thinly sliced
1 cup lightly packed fresh cilantro, chopped
2 limes, cut into wedges (optional)

1. Rinse beans with cold running water and discard any stones or shriveled beans. In large bowl, place beans and enough *water* to cover by 2 inches. Cover and let stand at room temperature overnight. (Or, in 6-quart saucepot, heat beans and enough *water* to cover by 2 inches to boiling over high heat; cook 2 minutes. Remove from heat; cover and let stand 1 hour.) Drain and rinse beans.

2. In 6-quart saucepot, heat oil over medium heat until hot. Add onions and cook, stirring occasionally, until tender, about 10 minutes. Add jalapeños, ginger, garlic, allspice, and thyme; cook, stirring, 3 minutes.

3. Add beans and water; heat to boiling over high heat. Reduce heat to low; cover and simmer 1 hour 30 minutes.

4. Add sweet potatoes, brown sugar, and salt; heat to boiling over high heat. Reduce heat to low; cover and simmer until beans and sweet potatoes are tender, about 30 minutes longer.

5. Transfer 1 cup bean mixture to blender; cover, with center part of lid removed to let steam escape, and puree until smooth.

6. Return puree to saucepot. Stir in green onions and cilantro. Serve with lime wedges, if you like.

Each serving: About 390 calories, 17g protein, 70g carbohydrate, 6g total fat (1g saturated), 0mg cholesterol, 705mg sodium.

Black-Bean Soup

This shortcut soup packs a genuine Tex-Mex wallop of flavor.

PREP: 10 MINUTES   COOK: 20 MINUTES

MAKES ABOUT 6 1/2 CUPS OR 4 MAIN-DISH SERVINGS

1 tablespoon vegetable oil
1 medium onion, finely chopped
2 garlic cloves, crushed with garlic
   press
2 teaspoons chili powder
1 teaspoon ground cumin
1/4 teaspoon crushed red pepper
2 cans (15 to 19 ounces each) black
   beans, rinsed and drained

1 can (14 to 14 1/2 ounces) chicken
   broth, or 1 3/4 cups Chicken Broth
   (page 74)
2 cups water
1/2 cup loosely packed fresh cilantro,
   chopped
lime wedges

1. In 3-quart saucepan, heat oil over medium heat until hot. Add onion and cook until tender, about 5 minutes. Stir in garlic, chili powder, cumin, and crushed red pepper; cook 30 seconds. Stir in beans, broth, and water; heat to boiling over high heat. Reduce heat to low; simmer, uncovered, 15 minutes.

2. Spoon half of mixture into blender; cover, with center part of cover removed to let steam escape, and puree until almost smooth. Pour into medium bowl. Repear with remaining mixture.

3. Return soup to same saucepan; heat through. Sprinkle with cilantro and serve with lime wedges.

Each serving: About 265 calories, 22g protein, 46g carbohydrate, 6g total fat (1g saturated), 0mg cholesterol, 965mg sodium.

Corn and Bean Chowder

This rich and creamy-looking soup—without a drop of cream—is easy to make, taking advantage of the convenience of canned beans and frozen corn.

PREP: 20 MINUTES   COOK: ABOUT 35 MINUTES
MAKES ABOUT 12 CUPS OR 12 FIRST-COURSE SERVINGS

2 tablespoons olive oil
3 medium carrots, cut lengthwise in half, then crosswise into 1/4-inch-thick slices
1 large stalk celery, cut lengthwise in half, then crosswise into 1/4-inch-thick slices
1 large onion (12 ounces), chopped
1 medium red pepper, cut into 1/2-inch pieces
2 packages (10 ounces each) frozen whole-kernel corn

2 cups water
2 cans (15 to 19 ounces each) pink beans, rinsed and drained
2 cans (14 to 14 1/2 ounces each) chicken broth, or 3 1/2 cups Chicken Broth (page 74)
1/2 teaspoon salt
1/4 teaspoon dried thyme
1/8 teaspoon ground red pepper (cayenne)

1. In 5- to 6-quart Dutch oven or saucepot, heat oil over medium heat until hot. Add carrots, celery, onion, and red pepper and cook, stirring frequently, until vegetables are tender-crisp, about 10 minutes.
2. Meanwhile, in blender, combine 1 package frozen corn with water and puree until almost smooth.
3. To Dutch oven, add pureed corn mixture, remaining package frozen corn, beans, broth, sugar, salt, thyme, and ground red pepper; heat to boiling over high heat. Reduce heat to low; cover and simmer, stirring occasionally, 20 minutes.

Each serving: About 140 calories, 6g protein, 25g carbohydrate, 4g total fat (1g saturated), 0mg cholesterol, 635mg sodium.

Do-ahead tip: Cool soup slightly and spoon into containers with tight-fitting lids. Refrigerate up to 2 days or freeze up to 1 month ahead. Reheat, without thawing, in Dutch oven, adding about 2 tablespoons water to pan to prevent scorching, or use the microwave.

Creamy Green Pea and Lettuce Soup

This lightly seasoned pureed soup is a great start to a Christmas feast. If you make the soup ahead and chill it, stir the lemon juice in after reheating.

PREP: 15 MINUTES   COOK: ABOUT 25 MINUTES

MAKES ABOUT 13 CUPS OR 12 FIRST-COURSE SERVINGS

1 tablespoon butter or margarine
1 large onion (12 ounces), finely chopped
2 cans (14 to 14 1/2 ounces each) chicken broth, or 3 1/2 cups Chicken Broth (page 74)
3 packages (10 ounces each) frozen peas
1 head Boston lettuce (about 10 ounces), coarsely chopped

3/4 teaspoon salt
1/4 teaspoon freshly ground black pepper
1/4 teaspoon dried thyme
2 cups water
2 cups whole milk
2 tablespoons fresh lemon juice
plain yogurt for garnish

1. In nonreactive 5- to 6-quart saucepot, melt butter over medium heat. Add onion and cook, stirring occasionally, until tender and lightly browned, 12 to 14 minutes. Stir in broth, frozen peas, lettuce, salt, pepper, thyme, and water; heat to boiling over medium-high heat. Reduce heat to low; simmer 5 minutes. Remove saucepot from heat; stir in milk.

2. Spoon one-fourth of mixture into blender; cover, with center part of lid removed to let steam escape, and puree until smooth. Pour puree into large bowl. Repeat with remaining mixture.

3. Return soup to same saucepot; heat through. Stir in lemon juice.

4. To serve, ladle soup into individual soup bowls and swirl some yogurt into each, if you like.

Each serving: About 105 calories, 6g protein, 14g carbohydrate, 3g total fat (1g saturated), 9mg cholesterol, 552mg sodium.

Split Pea Soup with Ham

On a wintry day, nothing satisfies more than an old-fashioned favorite like split pea soup.

PREP: 10 MINUTES   COOK: 1 HOUR 15 MINUTES
MAKES 11 CUPS OR 6 MAIN-DISH SERVINGS

2 tablespoons vegetable oil	1 package (16 ounces) split peas,
2 white turnips (6 ounces each),	rinsed and picked through
peeled and chopped (optional)	2 smoked ham hocks (1^1/$_2$ pounds)
2 medium carrots, peeled and finely	8 cups water
chopped	1 bay leaf
2 stalks celery, finely chopped	1 teaspoon salt
1 medium onion, finely chopped	^{1}/$_4$ teaspoon ground allspice

1. In 5-quart Dutch oven, heat oil over medium-high heat until hot. Add turnips, if using, carrots, celery, and onion; cook, stirring frequently, until carrots are tender-crisp, about 10 minutes. Add split peas, ham hocks, water, bay leaf, salt, and allspice; heat to boiling over high heat. Reduce heat; cover and simmer 45 minutes.

2. Remove and discard bay leaf. Transfer ham hocks to cutting board; discard skin and bones. Finely chop meat. Return meat to soup; heat through.

Each serving: About 343 calories, 21g protein, 52g carbohydrate, 7g total fat (1g saturated), 3mg cholesterol, 1,174mg sodium.

Curried Lentil Soup

Made with coriander, garlic, chopped apple, and served with a dollop of plain yogurt on top. Serve with toasted whole-wheat pitas.

PREP: 30 MINUTES   COOK: 1 HOUR

MAKES ABOUT 10 CUPS OR 5 MAIN-DISH SERVINGS

2 tablespoons olive oil
4 carrots, diced
2 large stalks celery, diced
1 large onion (12 ounces), chopped
1 medium Granny Smith apple,
    peeled, cored, and diced
1 tablespoon grated, peeled
    gingerroot
1 large garlic clove, crushed with
    garlic press
2 teaspoons curry powder
3/4 teaspoon ground cumin

3/4 teaspoon ground coriander
2 cans (14 to 141/2 ounces each)
    vegetable or chicken broth, or 31/2
    cups Vegetable Broth (page 16) or
    Chicken Broth (page 74)
1 package (16 ounces) lentils, rinsed
    and picked through
5 cups water
1/4 cup chopped fresh cilantro
1/2 teaspoon salt
plain low-fat yogurt

1. In 5-quart Dutch oven or saucepot, heat oil over medium-high heat until hot. Add carrots, celery, onion, and apple; cook, stirring occasionally, until lightly browned, 10 to 15 minutes.

2. Add ginger, garlic, curry, cumin, and coriander; cook, stirring, 1 minute.

3. Add broth, lentils, and water; heat to boiling over high heat. Reduce heat to low; cover and simmer, stirring occasionally, until lentils are tender, 45 to 55 minutes. Stir in cilantro and salt. Serve with yogurt.

Each serving without yogurt: About 370 calories, 20g protein, 60g carbohydrate, 7g total fat (1g saturated), 0mg cholesterol, 315mg sodium.

Lentil and Macaroni Soup

Another classic bowl of comfort. When served with crusty bread you'll have a meal—with enough left over to enjoy another day.

PREP: 20 MINUTES   COOK: ABOUT 50 MINUTES
MAKES ABOUT 12 CUPS OR 6 SERVINGS

1 tablespoon olive oil
2 medium carrots, cut into 1/4-inch pieces
1 medium onion, chopped
2 garlic cloves, crushed with garlic press
1 can (14 to 14 1/2 ounces) whole tomatoes in puree
1 can (14 to 14 1/2 ounces) vegetable broth or 2 cups Vegetable Broth (page 16)
3/4 cup lentils, rinsed and picked through

1/2 teaspoon salt
1/2 teaspoon coarsely ground black pepper
1/4 teaspoon dried thyme
6 cups water
1 bunch Swiss chard (about 1 pound), trimmed and coarsely chopped
3/4 cup elbow macaroni (about 3 1/2 ounces)
1 cup fresh basil, chopped
freshly grated Parmesan or Pecorino Romano cheese (optional)

1. In nonstick 5- to 6-quart Dutch oven, heat oil over medium heat until hot. Add carrots, onion, and garlic, and cook, stirring occasionally, until vegetables are tender and golden, about 10 minutes.

2. Add tomatoes with their puree, broth, lentils, salt, pepper, thyme, and water; heat to boiling, stirring to break up tomatoes with side of spoon. Reduce heat to low; cover and simmer until lentils are almost tender, about 20 minutes.

3. Stir in Swiss chard and macaroni; heat to boiling over medium-high heat. Reduce heat to medium; cook, uncovered, until macaroni is tender, about 10 minutes. Stir in basil. Serve with Parmesan, if you like.

Each serving: About 200 calories, 12g protein, 34g carbohydrate, 3g total fat (0g saturated), 0mg cholesterol, 810mg sodium.

Lentil and Bacon Soup

We chose lentils, one of the fastest-cooking dried legumes, and bacon, instead of a ham bone, for a hearty soup in a hurry.

PREP: 10 MINUTES   COOK: 30 MINUTES

MAKES ABOUT 9 CUPS OR 6 MAIN-DISH SERVINGS

1 bag (16 ounces) lentils (2½ cups), rinsed and picked through

1 carton (32 ounces) chicken broth, or 4 cups Chicken Broth (page 74)

2 bay leaves

4 cups water

4 slices bacon

1 medium onion, chopped

2 medium carrots, cut into ¼-inch-thick slices

2 medium stalks celery, cut into ¼-inch-thick slices

1 garlic clove, crushed with garlic press

1 teaspoon salt

¼ teaspoon freshly ground black pepper

¼ teaspoon dried thyme

1. In covered 4-quart saucepan, heat lentils, broth, bay leaves, and water to boiling over high heat. Reduce heat to low; simmer, covered, 15 minutes.

2. Meanwhile, in nonstick 12-inch skillet, cook bacon over medium-high heat until browned; transfer to paper towels to drain.

3. Discard all but 1 tablespoon drippings from skillet. Add onion, carrots, and celery, and cook, stirring occasionally, 5 minutes. Add garlic and cook, stirring, 1 minute longer.

4. Crumble bacon into lentil mixture; stir in salt, pepper, thyme, and vegetable mixture. Cover and cook until lentils are tender, about 5 minutes. Remove and discard bay leaves.

Each serving: About 335 calories, 24g protein, 48g carbohydrate, 6g total fat (2g saturated), 6mg cholesterol, 1,110mg sodium.

Lentil and Sausage Stew

You can substitute escarole, kale, or mustard greens for Swiss chard, but we love the striking red color of the chard.

PREP: 10 MINUTES   COOK: 20 MINUTES
MAKES ABOUT 7 CUPS OR 4 MAIN-DISH SERVINGS

1 bunch red Swiss chard (about
   1 pound), well rinsed
1 pound hot or mild Italian-sausage
   links, casings removed
2 small yellow summer squash (about
   6 ounces each)

2 small ripe plum tomatoes
1 can (19 ounces) ready-to-serve
   lentil soup
1 cup water

1. Cut Swiss chard stems into ¼-inch pieces; cut leaves into 1-inch-wide strips.

2. In 6-quart saucepot, cook sausages and chard stems over medium-high heat, breaking up sausages with side of spoon, until sausages are browned and stems are tender-crisp, about 10 minutes.

3. Meanwhile, trim ends and cut squash lengthwise in half, then crosswise into ¼-inch-thick slices. Chop tomatoes.

4. Increase heat to high. Add soup, squash, chard leaves, and water; cover and cook until squash is tender, about 5 minutes. To serve, top with tomatoes.

Each serving: About 490 calories, 23g protein, 22g carbohydrate, 35g total fat (12g saturated), 81mg cholesterol, 1,425mg sodium.

Vegetarian Lentil Stew

A hearty vegetarian option that's packed with fiber and low in sodium.

PREP: 10 MINUTES   COOK: ABOUT 20 MINUTES

MAKES ABOUT 6 1/4 CUPS OR 4 MAIN-DISH SERVINGS

2 teaspoons olive oil
2 teaspoons grated, peeled fresh
  ginger
2 garlic cloves, crushed with garlic
  press
2 teaspoons curry powder
1 package (1 pound) cut-up peeled
  butternut squash (about 4 cups),
  cut into bite-size pieces

1 large apple, unpeeled, cored, and
  cut into 1-inch pieces
1 can (19 ounces) ready-to-serve
  lentil soup
1/4 teaspoon salt
1 cup water
1 bag (10 ounces) prewashed
  spinach
lavash or pita (optional), toasted

1. In 4-quart saucepan, heat oil over medium heat until hot. Add ginger, garlic, and curry powder and cook, stirring, 30 seconds. Add squash, apple, soup, salt, and water; cover and heat to boiling over high heat. Reduce heat to medium; cook, covered, until squash is just tender, 5 minutes longer, stirring occasionally.

2. In batches, gently add as many spinach leaves as possible to lentil mixture, stirring to wilt spinach. Reduce heat to low; cover and simmer 5 minutes to blend flavors. Serve with lavash, if you like.

Each serving: About 190 calories, 9g protein, 34g carbohydrate, 4g total fat (0g saturated), 0mg cholesterol, 650mg sodium.

Sweet Potato and Black Bean Stew

A vegetable stew that's fragrant with orange and oregano. It's cooked in a pressure cooker, which allows you to have dinner on the table in minutes.

PREP: 20 MINUTES   COOK: 4 MINUTES PLUS BRINGING UP TO PRESSURE
MAKES ABOUT 8 CUPS OR 4 MAIN-DISH SERVINGS

1 orange
2 pounds sweet potatoes (about 4 medium), peeled and cut into 1¹/₂-inch pieces
2 cans (15 to 19 ounces each) black beans, rinsed and drained
1 can (14 to 14¹/₂ ounces) vegetable broth or chicken broth, or 1³/₄ cups Vegetable Broth (page 16) or Chicken Broth (page 74)

1 large onion (12 ounces), cut in half and thinly sliced
2 medium peppers (red and/or green), thinly sliced
2 garlic cloves, crushed with garlic press
¹/₂ teaspoon salt
¹/₂ teaspoon dried oregano
¹/₈ teaspoon crushed red pepper
1 cup loosely packed fresh cilantro, chopped

1. From orange, grate ¹/₂ teaspoon peel and squeeze 2 tablespoons juice.

2. In 6-quart pressure cooker, combine orange peel, sweet potatoes, beans, broth, onion, peppers, garlic, salt, oregano, and crushed red pepper. Following manufacturer's directions, cover pressure cooker, bring up to pressure, and cook under pressure 4 minutes. Release pressure quickly, as manufacturer directs. Stir in cilantro and orange juice.

Each serving: About 400 calories, 16g protein, 93g carbohydrate, 1g total fat (0g saturated), 0mg cholesterol, 1,305mg sodium.

CHILLED & FRUIT

Chilled Buttermilk and
Corn Soup, page 232

Gazpacho

This chilled soup of Spanish origin combines ripe tomatoes with other favorite veggies from the garden.

PREP: 30 MINUTES PLUS CHILLING

MAKES ABOUT 6 1/2 CUPS OR 6 FIRST-COURSE SERVINGS

2 medium cucumbers (about 8 ounces each), peeled and seeded
2 pounds ripe tomatoes (about 6 medium), seeded and chopped
1/2 medium red pepper, coarsely chopped
1 garlic clove, chopped
3 tablespoons fresh lemon juice
1 tablespoon olive oil

1 teaspoon salt
1/8 teaspoon coarsely ground black pepper
1/2 cup water
1 cup corn kernels cut from cobs (about 2 ears)
1 avocado, cut into 1/2-inch pieces
1/4 cup thinly sliced red onion

1. Cut 1 cucumber into 1/4-inch pieces; cut remaining cucumber into chunks.

2. Spoon half of tomatoes, red pepper, garlic, lemon juice, oil, salt, black pepper, cucumber chunks, and water into blender; puree until smooth. Pour into large bowl. Repeat with remaining half.

3. Stir in diced cucumber. Cover and refrigerate until well chilled, about 3 hours or overnight.

4. To serve, top soup with corn, avocado, and onion.

Each serving: About 145 calories, 3g protein, 19g carbohydrate, 8g total fat (1g saturated), 0mg cholesterol, 470mg sodium.

Gazpacho

Gazpacho with Cilantro Cream

Based on the popular uncooked soup from southern Spain, our chunky garden-fresh version is a welcome lunch or supper on hot days. Here, we've spiced up this summer treat by adding a jalapeño. Garnish with cilantro cream to cool the spice in the soup.

PREP: 30 MINUTES PLUS 6 HOURS OR OVERNIGHT TO CHILL

MAKES ABOUT 5 CUPS OR 4 FIRST-COURSE SERVINGS

2 medium cucumbers (about
  8 ounces each), peeled
1 medium yellow pepper
1/4 small red onion
2 pounds ripe tomatoes (about
  6 medium), peeled, seeded, and
  cut into 1/2-inch pieces
1/2 to 1 small jalapeño chile, seeded

3 tablespoons fresh lime juice
2 tablespoons extravirgin olive oil
3/4 plus 1/8 teaspoon salt
1/4 cup light sour cream or low-fat
  plain yogurt
1 tablespoon milk
5 teaspoons finely chopped fresh
  cilantro

1. Coarsely cut half of 1 cucumber, half of yellow pepper, and all of red onion; set aside. Cut remaining cucumbers and yellow pepper into chunks.

2. In food processor with knife blade attached, puree cucumber chunks, yellow pepper, tomatoes, jalapeño, lime juice, oil, and 3/4 teaspoon salt until smooth. Pour into medium bowl. Add cut-up cucumber, yellow pepper, and red onion. Cover and refrigerate until well chilled, at least 6 hours or overnight.

3. Meanwhile, prepare cilantro cream: In small bowl, mix sour cream, milk, 4 teaspoons chopped cilantro, and remaining 1/8 teaspoon salt until smooth. Cover and refrigerate until ready to serve soup.

4. Top each serving of cold soup with a dollop of cilantro cream and sprinkle with remaining chopped cilantro.

Each serving with cilantro cream: About 165 calories, 4g protein, 21g carbohydrate, 9g total fat (1g saturated), 6mg cholesterol, 505mg sodium.

Gazpacho with Cilantro Cream

Chilled Cucumber Soup

Homemade curry oil adds a taste of southeast Asia to this summer favorite.

PREP: 25 MINUTES PLUS CHILLING   COOK: 3 MINUTES
MAKES ABOUT 4 CUPS OR 4 FIRST-COURSE SERVINGS

CUCUMBER SOUP
2 English (seedless) cucumbers
  (about 12 ounces each), peeled
1 small garlic clove, crushed with
  garlic press
1 container (16 ounces) plain low-fat
  yogurt (about 2 cups)
1/2 cup low-fat (1%) milk
1 tablespoon fresh lemon juice
11/4 teaspoons salt

CURRY OIL
2 tablespoons olive oil
1/2 teaspoon curry powder
1/2 teaspoon ground cumin
1/4 teaspoon crushed red pepper

GARNISH
1 small tomato, chopped
1 tablespoon chopped fresh mint

1. Prepare soup: Cut enough cucumber into 1/4-inch pieces to equal 1/2 cup; reserve for garnish. Cut remaining cucumber into 1-inch pieces. In food processor with knife blade attached, or in blender, puree cucumber chunks, garlic, yogurt, milk, lemon juice, and salt until almost smooth. Pour mixture into medium bowl; cover and refrigerate until cold, about 2 hours.

2. Meanwhile, prepare curry oil: In small saucepan, heat oil, curry powder, cumin, and crushed red pepper over low heat until fragrant and oil is hot, about 3 minutes. Remove saucepan from heat; strain curry oil through sieve into cup.

3. Prepare garnish: In small bowl, combine tomato and reserved cucumber pieces.

4. To serve, stir soup and ladle into 4 bowls. Spoon cucumber mixture into center of soup. Sprinkle with mint and drizzle with curry oil.

Each serving: About 170 calories, 8g protein, 15g carbohydrate, 9g total fat (2g saturated), 8mg cholesterol, 830mg sodium.

Chilled Cucumber Soup

Vichyssoise

This luxurious soup, traditionally served cold, is just as delicious hot (just call it cream of potato and leek soup). Either way, serve in small cups and garnish with freshly chopped chives.

PREP: 20 MINUTES PLUS CHILLING   COOK: 55 MINUTES
MAKES ABOUT 8 CUPS OR 8 FIRST-COURSE SERVINGS

4 medium leeks (1 1/4 pounds)	1/2 cup water
2 tablespoons butter or margarine	1 teaspoon salt
1 pound all-purpose potatoes (3 medium), peeled and thinly sliced	1/4 teaspoon freshly ground black pepper
2 cans (14 to 14 1/2 ounces each) chicken broth, or 3 1/2 cups Chicken Broth (page 74)	1 cup milk
	1/2 cup heavy or whipping cream
	chives (for garnish)

1. Cut off roots and trim dark green tops from leeks; cut each leek lengthwise in half. Cut enough of white and pale green parts crosswise into 1/4-inch pieces to equal 4 1/2 cups. (Reserve any leftover leeks for another use.) Rinse leeks in large bowl of cold water, swishing to remove sand. Transfer to colander to drain, leaving sand in bottom of bowl.

2. In nonreactive 4-quart saucepan, melt butter over medium heat. Add leeks and cook, stirring occasionally, 8 to 10 minutes.

3. Add potatoes, broth, water, salt, and pepper; heat to boiling over high heat. Reduce heat; cover and simmer 30 minutes.

4. Spoon half of mixture into blender; cover, with center part of lid removed to let steam escape, and puree until smooth. Pour into bowl. Repeat with remaining mixture.

5. Stir milk and cream into puree. To serve hot, return soup to same clean saucepan and heat through over low heat (do not boil). To serve cold, cover and refrigerate at least 4 hours or until very cold. Garnish with chives before serving.

Each serving: About 161 calories, 4g protein, 14g carbohydrate, 10g total fat (7g saturated), 40mg cholesterol, 769mg sodium.

Chilled Buttermilk-Vegetable Soup

The refreshing, cool flavors of summer vegetables make this chunky soup a delightful first course.

PREP: 20 MINUTES PLUS CHILLING
MAKES ABOUT 10 CUPS OR 10 FIRST-COURSE SERVINGS

2 limes
1¹/₂ quarts buttermilk (6 cups)
3 medium tomatoes (about 1 pound),
  seeded and cut into ¹/₄-inch pieces
1 English (seedless) cucumber,
  unpeeled and cut into ¹/₄-inch
  pieces
1 ripe avocado, cut into ¹/₄-inch
  pieces

1 cup loosely packed fresh cilantro,
  chopped
1 teaspoon salt
¹/₄ teaspoon coarsely ground black
  pepper
fresh cilantro sprigs for garnish

1. From limes, grate 1 teaspoon peel and squeeze 3 tablespoons juice.
2. In large bowl, combine lime peel and juice, buttermilk, tomatoes, cucumber, avocado, cilantro, salt, and pepper and stir until blended. Cover and refrigerate at least 2 hours or up to 1 day. Garnish each serving with a cilantro sprig.

Each serving: About 105 calories, 6g protein, 11g carbohydrate, 4g total fat (1g saturated), 5mg cholesterol, 395mg sodium.

Chilled Buttermilk and Corn Soup

A quick and simple refrigerator soup—made with corn, tomatoes, cucumber, and basil—that's low-fat and satisfying.

PREP: 20 MINUTES PLUS CHILLING

MAKES ABOUT 4 1/2 CUPS OR 6 FIRST-COURSE SERVINGS

1 quart buttermilk
4 medium tomatoes, seeded and chopped (2 cups)
1 small cucumber, peeled, seeded, and chopped (1 cup)
2 cups corn kernels cut from cobs (3 to 4 ears)

1/2 teaspoon salt
1/4 teaspoon coarsely ground black pepper
12 large fresh basil leaves
2 small basil sprigs

1. In large bowl, stir buttermilk, tomatoes, cucumber, corn, salt, and pepper. Cover and refrigerate at least 2 hours or until very cold.
2. To serve, thinly slice basil leaves. Spoon soup into 6 bowls; garnish with sliced basil and basil sprigs.

Each serving: About 135 calories, 8g protein, 24g carbohydrate, 2g total fat (1g saturated), 6mg cholesterol, 365mg sodium.

Pear and Red Wine Soup

Serve this chilled soup before a hearty main course. As with all fruit soups, make it with fully ripened fruit at its peak of flavor.

PREP: 10 MINUTES PLUS CHILLING   COOK: 20 TO 25 MINUTES
MAKES ABOUT 3 1/2 CUPS OR 4 FIRST-COURSE SERVINGS

1 cup dry red wine	**1 lemon**
1 cup water	**1 1/2 pounds ripe pears, peeled,**
1/2 cup sugar	**cored, and cut into quarters**

1. In nonreactive 2-quart saucepan, heat wine, water, and sugar to boiling over high heat, stirring frequently, until sugar has dissolved.
2. Meanwhile, with vegetable peeler, from lemon, remove two 3-inch strips peel; squeeze 1 tablespoon juice.
3. Add pears and lemon peel to saucepan; heat to boiling over high heat. Reduce heat and simmer until pears are very tender, 10 to 15 minutes.
4. Spoon one-fourth of pear mixture into blender; cover, with center part of lid removed to let steam escape, and puree until smooth. Pour puree into bowl. Repeat with remaining mixture. Stir in lemon juice. Cover soup and refrigerate at least 4 hours or until very cold.

Each serving: About 234 calories, 1g protein, 50g carbohydrate, 1g total fat (0g saturated), 0mg cholesterol, 3mg sodium.

Peachy Melon Soup

Be sure to use the ripest, most fragrant melon you can find. The soup is also scrumptious garnished with slivers of prosciutto.

PREP: 15 MINUTES PLUS CHILLING

MAKES 5 FIRST-COURSE OR DESSERT SERVINGS

1 large cantaloupe (2 1/2 pounds), chilled
1 cup peach or apricot nectar

1 tablespoon fresh lime juice
lime slices

1. Cut cantaloupe in half. Remove and discard seeds. Cut away rind, then cut cantaloupe into bite-size pieces.
2. In blender, puree cantaloupe, peach nectar, and lime juice until smooth. Increase speed to high; blend 1 minute. If not serving right away, pour soup into bowl, cover, and refrigerate. To serve, garnish with lime slices.

Each serving: About 67 calories, 1g protein, 17g carbohydrate, 0g total fat (0g saturated), 0mg cholesterol, 14mg sodium.

Fruit Soup with Coconut Sorbet

Delightful at either the beginning *or* the end of a meal.

PREP: 10 MINUTES PLUS CHILLING
MAKES 4 CUPS OR 4 SERVINGS

1 lime
1 bottle (1 pint) passion fruit juice
  blend
2 tablespoons sugar
1 large ripe peach, peeled, pitted, and
  thinly sliced

1 red plum, pitted and thinly sliced
1/2 cup blueberries
1/2 cup raspberries
1 pint coconut, passion fruit, or
  mango sorbet
mint sprigs for garnish

1. From lime, grate 1/2 teaspoon peel and squeeze 2 tablespoons juice.
2. In medium bowl, toss lime peel and juice, fruit juice, sugar, peach, plum, blueberries, and raspberries until mixed. Cover and refrigerate at least 2 hours or until cold.
3. To serve, ladle fruit mixture into 4 shallow soup bowls. Top each with a scoop of sorbet. Garnish with mint sprigs.

Each serving: About 240 calories, 0g protein, 55g carbohydrate, 3g total fat (2g saturated), 0mg cholesterol, 40mg sodium.

INDEX

METRIC CONVERSION CHARTS

The recipes that appear in this cookbook use the standard United States method for measuring liquid and dry or solid ingredients (teaspoons, tablespoons, and cups). The information on this chart is provided to help cooks outside the U.S. successfully use these recipes. All equivalents are approximate.

METRIC EQUIVALENTS FOR DIFFERENT TYPES OF INGREDIENTS

A standard cup measure of a dry or solid ingredient will vary in weight depending on the type of ingredient. A standard cup of liquid is the same volume for any type of liquid. Use the following chart when converting standard cup measures to grams (weight) or milliliters (volume).

Standard Cup	Fine Powder (e.g., flour)	Grain (e.g., rice)	Granular (e.g., sugar)	Liquid Solids (e.g., butter)	Liquid (e.g., milk)
1	140 g	150 g	190 g	200 g	240 ml
$3/4$	105 g	113 g	143 g	150 g	180 ml
$2/3$	93 g	100 g	125 g	133 g	160 ml
$1/2$	70 g	75 g	95 g	100 g	120 ml
$1/3$	47 g	50 g	63 g	67 g	80 ml
$1/4$	35 g	38 g	48 g	50 g	60 ml
$1/8$	18 g	19 g	24 g	25 g	30 ml

USEFUL EQUIVALENTS FOR LIQUID INGREDIENTS BY VOLUME

$1/4$ tsp	=					1 ml
$1/2$ tsp	=					2 ml
1 tsp	=					5 ml
3 tsp	=	1 tbls	=		$1/2$ fl oz	=	15 ml
		2 tbls	=	$1/8$ cup	=	1 fl oz	=	30 ml
		4 tbls	=	$1/4$ cup	=	2 fl oz	=	60 ml
		$5 1/3$ tbls	=	$1/3$ cup	=	3 fl oz	=	80 ml
		8 tbls	=	$1/2$ cup	=	4 fl oz	=	120 ml
		$10 2/3$ tbls	=	$2/3$ cup	=	5 fl oz	=	160 ml
		12 tbls	=	$3/4$ cup	=	6 fl oz	=	180 ml
		16 tbls	=	1 cup	=	8 fl oz	=	240 ml
		1 pt	=	2 cups	=	16 fl oz	=	480 ml
		1 qt	=	4 cups	=	32 fl oz	=	960 ml
						33 fl oz	=	1000 ml	=	1 l

USEFUL EQUIVALENTS FOR DRY INGREDIENTS BY WEIGHT

(To convert ounces to grams, multiply the number of ounces by 30.)

1 oz	=	$1/16$ lb	=	30 g
4 oz	=	$1/4$ lb	=	120 g
8 oz	=	$1/2$ lb	=	240 g
12 oz	=	$3/4$ lb	=	360 g
16 oz	=	1 lb	=	480 g

USEFUL EQUIVALENTS FOR COOKING/OVEN TEMPERATURES

	Fahrenheit	Celsius	Gas Mark
Freeze Water	32° F	0° C	
Room Temperature	68° F	20° C	
Boil Water	212° F	100° C	
Bake	325° F	160° C	3
	350° F	180° C	4
	375° F	190° C	5
	400° F	200° C	6
	425° F	220° C	7
	450° F	230° C	8
Broil			Grill

USEFUL EQUIVALENTS FOR LENGTH

(To convert inches to centimeters, multiply the number of inches by 2.5.)

1 in	=			2.5 cm
6 in	=	$1/2$ ft	=	15 cm
12 in	=	1 ft	=	30 cm
36 in	=	3 ft	= 1 yd	=	90 cm
40 in	=			100 cm = 1 m